MY RISKY ROMANCE
IN TURKEY

A TRUE STORY

KAREN CARLSON

BOOKSIDE Press

BOOKSIDE Press

BookSide Press
877-741-8091
www.booksidepress.com
orders@booksidepress.com

CONTENTS

DEDICATION

For my husband, and in memory
of my parents and sister

PROLOGUE

I was very tired, just completely exhausted. The events of the day had been a huge shock to me. In fact, the previous months had been anything but relaxing. I just wanted to lie down and sleep and sleep.

I washed my face at the washbasin, walked into that strange room, and climbed up to the bed (at least that's what they called the wooden tables there). I stretched out on the scratchy blanket and covered myself with the sheet that I'd been lent.

And I slept.

But it wasn't too long before I began to wake up. I was very hot, very uncomfortable. I tried to shift my body into a better position, but I felt confined. Why? I only wanted to turn onto my stomach, but I was too cramped to do so. Why? Again, I slept.

But hours later, or so it seemed, I awoke again. Now I was soaking wet. Drops of sweat slithered down my face, under my arms. *No, no, no, I have to sleep,* I thought, half-conscious. *But why am I so hot? Why am I dressed? What am I wearing anyway?* My fingers grasped that clammy wet thing I was wearing.

What is this? Why am I sleeping in my clothes?

I had slept nude since I'd been a child.

Why was I dressed now? Or was this a nightgown? I didn't own one.

Questions and answers raced through my mind. Nothing made sense.

My heart began pumping hard. My hands trembled. Fear! I was really afraid. *Could it be? Could it have happened to me? No, it's impossible.* Frightening thoughts were everywhere. I felt like I was going crazy.

Panic began to overtake me.

Just go to sleep. Just try to sleep. It's only a nightmare. Sleep, I ordered myself.

Keeping my eyes closed and trying to relax, I tried to doze off. I felt a little better now. But not for long.

This time I really awoke. Now I was wide awake, breathing in short spurts.

No, this isn't a nightmare. Not at all, I told myself. *My God! This is real. This is happening to me. Oh my God! What am I going to do?*

My eyes open, I let myself look around me.

There was nothing to see. There was no light at all. I was terrified now. I shut my eyes again and did my best to fight my fear and growing sense of claustrophobia.

I knew I should relax, daydream about lying on a beach, listening to good music, and being happy.

But instead of hearing ocean waves, I could hear people breathing, someone snoring. I knew I was in that room, that awful place I'd seen. I knew the only way I could survive would be to sleep again, as long as I could.

Instead of sleeping, though, I became more terrified. My breathing sped up. My whole body was shaking now. The place was pitch-dark. It was also filled with sleeping bodies. I was surrounded. I couldn't breathe now. I was going to die. Claustrophobia!

Finally, I remembered everything that had happened. I realized now what was going on. This was truly real. My entire being reacted.

The truth was that I was stuck. There was nothing I could do about it. I couldn't just leave. I realized there was no one to help me. I couldn't really converse with anyone in that place. I couldn't even contact the people in the village for help. But most of all, I couldn't get out of that room to the outside. Not only that, but also I couldn't even look outside. Never in my life had I felt like that. It was a hell on earth. The feeling was too awesome to cry about. It was like an immense wall of fear and tightness growing inside me. I fought for control of myself because I knew if I let go, I'd begin screaming and drive myself insane.

At long last, I forced myself to close my eyes and cease all thought. It was a battle I was fighting with myself. I tried to calm myself. But that tightness persisted.

After what seemed like hours, somehow my sanity won over and I finally fell asleep.

But nothing had changed. I was still there. And there was nothing that I could do about it.

I had ruined my life.

CHAPTER 1

I grew up in Urbana, Illinois, a university town. My father and most of my friends' fathers were professors. It was just assumed that my friends and I would go on to the university. In my case, while I already knew that I would graduate from college, all that meant to me was that "everyone else does this; it's just part of growing up." Not really serious about being a college student, I just had a good time. Managing to get by with little study, I graduated with a bachelor's degree in child development.

I had a great family, including one sister, who was younger than I. My parents had a very loving marriage. I never heard them fight; on the contrary, it seemed to me they were always hugging and kissing. I grew up believing that all marriages were like theirs.

Because of my childhood, I developed a lifelong wanderlust. My family spent a large part of each summer on the road (not the interstates but the old two-lane highways of this country). While traveling, the four of us camped every night in tents in the national parks and other campgrounds. By the time I became an adult, I had seen, and really felt I knew a lot about, most of the fifty states. After university, I spent three months in Europe, using a Eurail pass to get around and explore most of the countries. Traveling was something I thought everyone did. And probably because of how I was brought up, I became a traveler who experimented with and tried to adopt different cultures. I tended to immerse myself in any new environment and tried to learn as much about the people and their lives as I could. For me, travel became my true means of education.

I had been a boy-crazy girl since I could remember, but when I began dating, each of my relationships with a boyfriend was long term and faithful—and then I became interested in someone else. At that point, I would break up with the present boyfriend and switch to the new one. It is well known now that remaining a virgin was the thing to do in the 1950s. I managed to remain one technically until halfway through the university. Even then, the quick sex I had with my boyfriend was in the backseat of a car. And since neither of us had regular use of a car, we rarely got to partake of this pleasure. The reason behind my first marriage was this: I truly wanted to spend the night with my lover and have legal sex—and anyway, getting married was the thing to do when you finished university, wasn't it? Not many women seriously thought of careers in the 1950s. So by the time I graduated, I also was a new wife.

I tried to make things work with Dick, my husband. I really did. He adored me. He was a good man, a good husband. There was nothing wrong with the marriage, but I had married far too young (for me, that is). Looking back on it, I realize my behavior toward being married was one of playing at being an adult, playing house.

Dick went to grad school and, after receiving his PhD, took a job in Washington. I did temporary jobs once in a while, got bored, and started feeling trapped. Dick seemed more and more conservative to me. I longed to be with a man who'd be more lively and fun-loving.

Then one day, I met a guy at the pool in our apartment complex. Cap was a good-looking hippie who lived in the complex. He was tall, dark, and slender and had a gorgeous head of long, shiny black hair. He was drifting at the time, having dropped out of school. I was wildly attracted to him and his rebelliousness. We got along well and enjoyed doing things together, such as riding around on his motorcycle and attending rock concerts. He was, I thought, a great contrast to conservative Dick. Cap and I seemed to be well matched. Plus, the romance was new and exciting. We became lovers.

After a few weeks of this affair, I moved out of the apartment I shared with Dick and into Cap's apartment. It was winter in Washington; there had just been one of the biggest snowstorms in history. Following my lifelong passion for travel, and also longing for some sun and warmth,

I suddenly thought, *Why don't Cap and I go somewhere?* Each of us had some savings, and we were both unemployed. Cap was really enthusiastic about the idea. Within a week, we were on our way to Greece, a warm place that neither of us had seen before.

CHAPTER 2

January 1970

The trip began very easily. Cap's brother, Brian, drove us to the Greyhound bus terminal in Washington, DC. After a quick ride to New York, we arrived at the Port Authority and quickly got lost. No one seemed to know where to catch the airport bus. Even though we were still in our own country and English was our language, we felt like we were already in a foreign place since we had so much trouble communicating with all the immigrant people who worked at the Port Authority. Eventually, though, we found our way to the airport bus, just barely making it to the Icelandic Airlines terminal in time.

Our airline of choice had been Icelandair, the airline that offered the cheapest rates for flights to Luxembourg, combined with a free overnight stopover at a hotel in Reykjavik, Iceland, and a sightseeing tour. Once we arrived at the terminal, it was obvious to me that young travelers and hippies had taken advantage of the prices. Not one "old person" or conservative-looking "straight" person was around. Everyone was dressed in jeans or trendy casual clothing. When I'd first gone to Europe in 1966, everyone dressed up for plane travel. Not anymore, at least not in this age group.

When our plane took off late, it took forever for the thing to get off the ground and climb to its cruising altitude. It seemed like we were hanging around at the height of the tallest buildings for a very long time, and there was a tense mood among all the passengers. Would we really make it?

Partly because of the odd takeoff and partly because the plane was filled with hippies, there was lots of hash smoking on the flight, and joints were being passed around, much to Cap's excitement. Having tried smoking grass only twice before with no noticeable effect, I didn't find the idea of smoking very appealing. So I didn't have any, even though Cap tried to convince me to do so.

"Come on, babe," he urged. "Give it a try. This is really great shit."

"No, not here. Later. I promise," I replied, leaning back against the seat and closing my eyes. "I just want to relax now."

Cap looked puzzled. "But this is by far the best way to relax," he replied, disgusted.

After a few more attempts to persuade me, he gave up. Soon, he was so stoned that he didn't care if I smoked or not.

After a long, smoked-filled flight, we landed at Keflavik International Airport in Iceland. Cap and I took a bus to Reykjavik. We'd earlier decided to take advantage of the stopover plan and the sightseeing in Iceland, but we ended up seeing virtually nothing of that country. The hotel where we stayed did offer a chance to enjoy a delicious smorgasbord with a large concentration of fish. After a swim in the hotel pool and an afternoon nap to rest up from the sleepless night, we were visited by some of our fellow travelers from the flight who were staying over too. They came bringing hashish. We all got stoned—yes, this time I decided to smoke some. The hash they had was really strong and affected me quickly. Being so ignorant, I just didn't realize how much I was smoking, but I kept up with everyone, taking some every time it was passed around. After an hour of smoking, we decided to go have dinner, so I got up from the bed where I'd been sitting and went into our room to get my shoes. I knew I'd smoked too much then; everything was in a haze. Dreaming, floating, separate in mind and body, and trying to coordinate my vision, thoughts, and actions, I went with the others down to the dining room of the hotel.

As we walked in, everybody in the dining room turned and looked at us. Of course, we weren't dressed like they were. They were in suits and nice dinner dresses, whereas we were in jeans and minidresses.

All the guys in our group had long hair. Even though the stares were warranted, the hash was beginning to make me paranoid and I was terribly uncomfortable. We found a large table in the corner. I took a seat facing the room. Distances were distorted to me; the room seemed to stretch on and on. When the table was pushed toward me to make room for the others on the opposite side, I felt like they'd pushed it a mile. Faces looked at me from the distance. I began to get scared. This couldn't be real. Actually, this was the first time that smoking had affected me to any great extent, but I had no way of knowing that beforehand. I had a lot to learn, and this experience was going to teach me. I don't remember eating my soup, but afterward Cap said I had. Whole pieces of conversations seemed to be missing. A couple of times, I grabbed Cap's leg and tried to convey my fear of what was happening. For a while, I felt I was in the room with everyone at a distance, and then I would mentally leave, come back later, and have no idea what had happened. It was terrifying.

Near the end of the meal, I tried to pick up my fork but couldn't manage it. I tried to tell Cap that I was thirsty, but my voice wouldn't work; finally I squeaked out that I wanted some water. When the water was brought to me, no matter how I tried, I couldn't lift my arm to take hold of the glass. I panicked. Again, I tried to attract Cap's attention. He seemed very far away. "Help!" I tried to say, but not a sound came out of my mouth. I was positive I had gone insane.

Finally, Cap, who was very stoned himself, upon realizing what was happening to me, suggested we leave. Somehow I made it out of the dining room with him and to the elevator. Once on the elevator with him alone, I let go of all my fears and started shaking violently. Cap was scared, but not half as much as I was. Once he got me into our room, I fell on the bed and began crying loudly. At intervals, I mentally left the room, and then I would come back and realize that Cap was there holding me down and trying to convince me that I was all right. He suggested that I just give it time, saying that the effects of the drug would wear off. At one point our new friends appeared at the door. I was aware of Cap's telling them that there was no problem.

Later on that same night, after the effects of the hash had worn off, all of us went out to a discotheque, a huge place with three floors and a band on each. The beautiful young Icelandic women were attracted to Cap and were very aggressive, much to his pleasure. Since the Icelandic men were also quite flirtatious, the entire group met lots of people that night. After a few hours of dancing and talking, we left the disco with an Icelandic man, Cap's new friend. We ended up in his small room. Everyone smoked again, except for me. I had learned my lesson from my earlier experience—for that night, anyway.

Early the next morning, we awoke in the dark and left Iceland at ten in the morning, still in the dark. Iceland has those long winter nights and long summer days. I haven't said much about Iceland because I certainly didn't see much while we were there. Since we'd slept in the afternoon, we'd missed the tour around the city that the airline offered for free. At least we did have a quick look at the landscape on the way to and from the airport. At that time of year, there was no vegetation. Since the ground was covered with snow and the houses and buildings were wood and very plain, everything looked drab and colorless.

The flight from Iceland to Luxembourg was uneventful. We landed in the early evening, went through immigration and customs, and then made our way into town. Our first destination in Europe was Venice, which I had thought Cap would like because of his Italian heritage. So we checked the train schedules and found that there was an overnight train to Venice, leaving that evening at nine. To pass the time until the train arrived, we found a restaurant and had dinner.

By the time we got to Venice the next day, we were very tired. We hadn't had a good night's sleep since starting our trip. We found a nice hotel very near to St. Mark's Square and spent a lazy day walking around the city and resting in the room. While exploring Venice, we met a young Australian woman whom Cap invited to tag along with us for the whole day. He seemed very dependent on having lots of people around him. This was something I hadn't noticed about him while in the States.

When we returned to our hotel room, Cap claimed he had a fever and started acting childish and bitchy. The weather was cold and rainy, but Cap's real and main complaint was that there was no hash available. Our little trip, the trip that we'd planned to be romantic and perfect, was starting out to be exactly the opposite. Here was another thing about

Cap that seemed to have changed almost immediately after starting to travel. He'd always loved grass, but in just a short time, he seemed to have acquired a constant need for it. I started wondering how he could be in a place like Venice, very picturesque and interesting even in the rain, and complain that he had no hash. And he seemed to have no patience when things weren't perfect for him.

Our original travel plan had been to take a boat to Athens from Brindisi, an Italian port. Whereas some travel agencies said there was a boat at this time of year, others disagreed. Finally we decided to take a train, since we knew for sure they existed. The following day we bought overnight train tickets to Athens. Cap had seen enough of Venice, and both of us were now anxious to leave the chilly weather behind us.

The trip from Venice to Athens via Yugoslavia was a long and mostly boring one. The train seemed to crawl along for the two nights and a day it took to arrive. In one Yugoslavian town, passengers were supposed to change trains, but we hadn't been told (or at least Cap and I hadn't heard anything about it, probably because it hadn't been announced in English). At the last minute, a conductor came along and motioned us off the train. Down the tracks we ran. Cap had been shooting home movies. When putting the camera back in the bag, he had failed to zip it up. I was carrying the bag and didn't notice it was open. Of course, the camera fell out and bounced on the concrete pavement. This put Cap into a furious mood for the rest of the trip.

"Why didn't you check to see if the bag was zipped?" he screamed at me.

"And why didn't you remember to zip it up?" I replied, furious.

From the beginning of our trip, Cap had started being childish and moody. Now, after only a few days, it seemed everything bad that happened was entirely my fault.

February 4, 1970

Yugoslavia continued to be cold, dreary, and snowy. The people I saw from the train window were dressed in dark clothing, and everything looked totally depressing. How I was looking forward to Greece, sun, and warm weather. Slowly, as the train crawled along and we approached the Greek border, signs of spring started to appear. The snow began to vanish and we could see flowers in bloom. What anticipation. Even Cap began to get excited.

Our compartment-mate, a little Yugoslavian man, wanting to be friends apparently, insisted on sharing his food with us. We politely refused, but since he continued to offer, we finally accepted. This was our first introduction to the constant offering of things to strangers by people in Greece and Turkey. The few months in my life that I've smoked cigarettes began on that train ride, because I was offered one—and once I had taken it, I couldn't refuse having it lighted. Even a polite refusal wasn't accepted by those people.

At last, we arrived in Athens. The buildings were white and the city was spread out. The sun was shining and it was warm. Cap and I were ecstatic. The Australian woman in Venice had recommended the Lido Hotel, so we took a bus to Omonia Square. But we hadn't anticipated having so much trouble finding the hotel. The square was very crowded, and lots of little streets branched off it. The Lido was on one of these offshoot streets. After what seemed like ages, we finally found the place and got settled in.

The Lido was modern and clean, and we had our own bath. Nevertheless, by the time we were settled there, Cap was in a foul mood.

"Why are you wearing that ugly trench coat?" he complained.

Cap loved my trench coat, but he had used it as a pillow on the train. Now, since it had been used as a pillow, he decided it shouldn't be worn anymore. In truth, the coat was still clean and didn't even look wrinkled. I was getting tired of his bursts of irrationality, which were becoming more and more common. Why couldn't he start to enjoy himself? After all, we were finally in Athens and the weather was beautiful. Who cared if my trench coat had been used as a pillow?

Immediately after putting his backpack in the closet, Cap went down to the hotel lobby, hoping to meet some "freaks." However, soon he reappeared and announced that he was starving. Then he threw a screaming fit until we got ready to find a place to eat. After this episode, we carried food for him whenever we went out to avoid his starvation and the resultant temper tantrums. Luckily that day, we saw a restaurant across the street from the hotel. We ordered moussaka, a casserole dish made of ground lamb and eggplant in layers and topped with béchamel sauce. This turned out to be our favorite Greek dish. It was delicious. Cap was happy again, and so was I.

After lunch, we decided to walk to the Parthenon. After arriving in Athens, I had changed from my jeans, sweater, and boots to a sleeveless jumper with blouse and sandals. The sun felt very good. Halfway up to the Parthenon, I went behind a bush and took off my blouse—all the better to catch the sun.

Finally, I was enjoying the day, the weather, and Athens, and Cap was in a better mood, but still not satisfied. He kept wanting to find some hash.

"Everything would be perfect if I had some shit," he kept telling me.

At the top of the Acropolis, he saw some hippies and immediately introduced himself. We spent the rest of the day with these two Englishmen who had been teaching English in Greece. Although they didn't have any hash with them, they told Cap they could locate some—which they did. The three of them then spent the afternoon discussing ways of carrying shit across international borders. I amused myself by sitting on the rocks sunning myself, ignoring their conversation and enjoying the view of Athens from the Parthenon. They talked excitedly all afternoon. Cap smoked with his two new friends and, as usual, dominated the conversation. Remembering the bad experience I'd had in Iceland with the hash, I refused to smoke.

Late that afternoon, Cap, his new British friends, and I made our way back down the hills and into the Plaka, the old section of Athens. This was an interesting section of the city, mostly filled with nightclubs, tourist shops, and restaurants. I was enticed by all the things to buy, especially the colorful pottery plates. At the end of the Plaka, we split from the others and went back to our section of town, Omonia Square. Cap was hungry again, so we went to find a restaurant. One of the hippie travelers on the streets recommended a souvlakia stand, so we searched for one of those.

The traveler knew what he was talking about. Souvlakia was a delicious treat. For twelve cents we got a great sandwich. For souvlakia, lamb is roasted on a spit and then thinly sliced. These slices are stuffed into pita bread and covered with tzatziki sauce, tomatoes, and onions.

Eating souvlakia quickly became our habit; we ate it for snacks and meals at all hours of the day and night.

Both of us were dying to taste baklava, a sweet Greek dessert, so went to a pastry shop and bought a box of pastries—baklava and *kadaif*. We then returned to the hotel lobby, because Cap was hoping to meet some more hippies. But instead of meeting hippies, we met some Nigerians, with whom we spent the evening. They were fascinating people. At the end of the evening, we left with their addresses and invitations to visit them in Africa.

The next day was beautiful and sunny, so Cap and I decided to find a beach. After all, we had come to Greece to escape Washington's winter and to spend time on the Greek beaches. We took a bus out to the highway that runs along the sea and then caught another bus heading east. Since we had no idea where to go, we tried to communicate with the Greeks on the bus about which beach to choose. One pointed to the next stop, so we got off. There was definitely a beach there—white, sandy, deserted—and the water was clear and turquoise. The only flaw was tar. Everywhere. Still, it was a quiet, relaxing day, just like we had originally planned.

The next day, searching for another, cleaner beach, we took the bus line out of town and through some little villages. A Scandinavian couple was in the bus this time. They said they were looking for the same kind of place we were, deserted. I was aware at once that they wanted to be alone, but Cap, very dependent on people, wanted to spend the afternoon with them, so he latched on. We all got off at the same spot and looked for a place on the rocky and sandy coast there. I kept feeling that these people wanted to be on their own and kept trying to get Cap to leave. Finally he agreed, when he at last sensed the same thing.

Cap and I then found our little spot on the rocks. We had a good time sunning ourselves. It was such a gorgeous day. After a few hours, we decided to hitchhike back to Athens instead of waiting for the bus. Our first ride was in the closed-in back of a truck. The driver and his companions gave us cheese and bread to eat. Our second ride was in a car, whose driver tried to carry on a conversation with us in Greek. Since we didn't know even one Greek word, it was pretty silly. He kept persisting with one question, and finally pulled up to a pastry shop and motioned us in. What he had been asking was whether or not we'd like a snack. Of course we would, and it certainly was good—baklava and cakes, coffee, tea. All on him. We were quite impressed with his generosity, the same penchant for giving that we were finding all over.

That evening, we decided to go find Cap's English friend at his place at Syntagma Square. He was staying at a pension that was in that vicinity, but on a side street. Cap found it with the directions he'd been given. The pension was like a commune—all hippies, mostly European. We sat around and drank and talked, finally taking off for a discotheque. Since Cap was spending most of his time with the British man and paying no attention to me, I enjoyed myself talking to a nice Dutch guy. The discotheque was enjoyable—Greek music and rock, and both kinds of dancing.

We met the same group of men the next day at their pension and decided to go visit the US Sixth Fleet. It was a cloudy day, so the beach wouldn't be a good choice, but still I wasn't too happy with the plans. *Who wants to visit a US Navy fleet while in Greece?* I thought. It seemed absurd, but I was outnumbered. At the port, a sailor showed us around. While on the boats, we noticed that there was oil in the water everywhere, great pools of it. It was foul. The sailor insisted that the oil wasn't from the Sixth Fleet. *Sure,* I thought. That night we had some great Greek food at a little restaurant and then went to our room with the guys. They all smoked.

Lots of European people were around us, constantly smoking. I continued to feel more and more isolated and lonely, even though surrounded by people. Although still physically with me, Cap was off on a trip of his own now.

The next morning, Cap and I decided we'd had enough of Athens and decided to go to Crete. Actually, it wasn't really the islands Cap was interested in, but the camp of hippies living in caves at Matala that he'd been told about. The idea of living in caves with hippies didn't appeal to me at all, but I wasn't against the idea of going to a Greek island, so I agreed. We packed up and took the commuter train to the port of Piraeus. The boat left in the evening and traveled overnight.

We bought deck-class tickets and afterward were a little sorry we had, even though it was the cheapest way to travel. At first the boat staff wanted to separate the passengers according to gender when assigning sleeping places. There were two sets of small rooms with bunk beds. They wanted the men to go on one side and the women on the other. But there were many young people in deck class, and many couples, so this little rule of theirs didn't hold. The guys moved to the women's side. At one point during the evening, Cap and I decided to try to sneak into the class above us; they were showing a movie up there, and the accommodations looked very comfortable, compared to our wooden benches and bunks. We made it into the living room section, but when Cap tried to cash a traveler's check there, the staff, deciding he looked like a deck-class type, showed us the way back downstairs.

The ride was smooth and comfortable, and it was beautiful outside at night. However, the bunks were really uncomfortable. Plus, in our room another couple was really going at it sexually. I would have been embarrassed in their place. They were Greeks. Cap periodically yelled at them in English to shut up. Of course that did no good.

After a rather unusual night of listening to sex instead of doing it ourselves, we landed in Iraklion, a medium-sized town, and found a pension right away. The pension was built around a courtyard and was pretty nice. Compared to the Lido, it was much simpler and, happily, much cheaper.

We spent the afternoon exploring the town. In the marketplace, we both were shocked beyond words when we came upon dead sheep and goats hanging up for sale. To us, meat was sold in packages in the supermarkets. In the United States, it was easy to overlook the fact that we were buying dead animals. Recovering from that shock, we were really interested in the little shops in the area and the city in general. Everything was whitewashed and beautiful. We ended up in a tiny coffee shop at the edge of town near the sea, drinking tea and wine. The village men liked Cap and followed their custom, buying him wine and more wine, which he didn't refuse. We sat at a table on the sidewalk outside, where I basked in the sun. On the way back to the room, Cap bought each of us a Greek bag; he insisted on making the choice of colors. His was woven with bright colors; mine was beige and brown (I was a bit envious since I preferred his—and he knew it.)

Despite the problems we were having with Cap's tantrums, moodiness, and constant looking for drugs, we were still carrying on our love affair. Having heard about youth hostels, we decided not to stay in one since they separated the sexes and we wanted to sleep together. However, as usual, Cap wanted to meet some people, so we went to the hostel in town that night, met some people right away, and ended up going with them to a party at a Greek man's place in the suburbs. Since we had to go by bus, we found out that we'd have to return to town by one in the morning since the last bus left at that time. The party wasn't too bad—lots of drinks and music. I spent most of the evening talking to the Greek host of the party, who was very good-looking and rich. With Cap always carried away on his highs and meeting other freaks, I decided there was no reason I should just sit in a corner, so I didn't. We stayed at the party so long that we almost missed the last bus back into town.

The next morning we decided to go to Matala, so we went into the town center and tried to find out where and when to catch the afternoon bus. We spent the rest of the day waiting at a coffee shop right in the center of town that was frequented by freaks and Greeks alike. I was wearing a minidress. One young woman I met told me that it was nice, but not at all the kind of thing to wear to Matala.

"All they wear there is jeans and old clothing," she said. "Wear something worn and torn there."

There were lots of tales of Matala. It seemed everyone had been there. Some had stayed for months.

The bus finally arrived. The ride to Matala was fascinating. We crossed the island, going from the northern side to the southern. The bus first climbed the mountainous spine of central Crete and then descended onto a large plain. The other passengers were villagers with their chickens, baskets, and huge packages. It was noisy and interesting. I had never seen such picturesque villages. Because the roads were so narrow, the bus barely made it into a couple of small towns and had a difficult time turning around. Chickens and donkeys were everywhere. We encountered little old women dressed in black, and men in baggy bloomer-type trousers. It was another world for me, so it was surprising how soon this all seemed to be commonplace. At the end of the bus route, only a few of us—all young travelers—were left.

Matala is a tiny village in a cove enclosed by bluffs of age-old packed earth in which humans—possibly beginning under the Romans but most likely no earlier than AD 500—have dug chambers, some complete with bunk beds. These cave-like rooms were first used by the people of Greece as summer homes; then German soldiers used them as storerooms during World War II; and now the hippies were living in them.

As we entered Matala, we saw hippies everywhere. I had earlier told Cap that I really didn't want to stay in a cave, a communal thing, and he had promised we'd stay in the town's only tiny hotel. What a horrible place it was! Damp, wet, cold, and miserable, with uncomfortable beds and a dirty outhouse. Several other people were staying in the hotel at the time because there weren't any vacancies in the caves.

We spent five days in Matala. The days were lazy; not much was going on. Lots of hours were spent on the beach, soaking up the sun and swimming. Time was spent visiting people in their caves, drinking and eating at one or another of the tiny restaurants, and dancing at night at a little bar–restaurant. There was a jukebox in the bar with mostly Greek music and a couple of rock songs, including Led Zeppelin's latest hit, which was played over and over.

Matala had been a quiet village until the kids found the caves. When that happened, the villagers, deciding to take advantage of the opportunity to make some money, opened the tiny hotel and another restaurant. Now even though far from a modern or commercialized place, Matala had been spoiled. I felt it very sad that the villagers' quiet lives had been disrupted.

Most of the travelers in Matala were European—lots of Dutch, Germans, Scandinavians, and English. There were also some Australians and New Zealanders, and a few Americans. Cap and I made friends with another American couple who had rented a tiny two-room house in the village. The house was barren, had no plumbing or kitchen, and was entirely absent of furniture. Our friends were sleeping in their sleeping bags on the floor. They had dug a hole in their backyard and covered it with a board for a toilet seat—all in clear view of the nearby shepherds.

In contrast to that house, the caves were quite livable. Most of them had at least two rooms and were fixed up elaborately by the travelers. The ledges along the sides of the walls had originally been burial places, but the bodies had long since disappeared. To where? No seemed to know. These ledges now served as bench-style seats and often beds. All the caves had some type of kitchen setup with gas hot plates or burners. Of course, water had to be carried up from the well in the center of the village, which must have been a real chore, since it was quite a climb to some of the caves. Actually, I was amazed when I saw that most of the caves were quite impressive, comfortable, and homey. However, not so impressive were the outside ledges that passed by the caves. Although there were public showers and toilets in the village, the ledges outside the caves were often used instead. As a result, they smelled and looked terrible.

Matala had the oddest assortment of young people that I'd ever seen in one group—anywhere. There were those few who appeared to be fairly conservative, but they were rare and usually didn't stay long. The strange thing was that there was no hash or other drugs around. Everyone was drinking instead. We heard through the grapevine that the Greek authorities had been watching the place closely.

One particularly strange traveler had been in Matala for years, people said. He was Dutch and very tall, and no matter what the temperature, he always wore a long dark woolen coat that was huge. He never talked to anyone. The only thing people knew about him was what other people had guessed. I'm not sure how he survived, except that every night he appeared in the restaurant where we were eating and just stood there and held out his hand. Even though most of the hippies there followed their philosophy of giving, people were really irritated by this man. Yet enough people fed him that he obviously got by.

Another weird character in Matala was an American man, a religious fanatic. He was a southerner and looked like a freak, but he was insanely religious. Cap got into some heated arguments and almost fought physically with him a couple of times.

One wonderful thing about the village was the fresh-baked bread that appeared every morning. At the time I thought it was the best bread I'd ever tasted. We'd buy some butter and spread it on the thick warm slices. Each morning there was a group of people waiting anxiously for that bread to be taken out of the oven.

After we had stayed in Matala for five days, Cap and I noticed that both of us seemed to have a tolerance limit for staying in one place. We'd spent five days in Athens and were anxious to leave; now we were ready to leave Matala. There was a problem, though. The bus only came in a couple of days a week. We weren't sure if the day we hoped to leave would be one of those days. But we were lucky. The bus did show up on the day we decided to go, a dreary, miserable day.

We had no certain plans about where to go next, but Cap had the idea of going to Rhodes, another Greek island. Some people had been talking about it, and it seemed the logical next move since boats were going from Crete to Rhodes daily. When we arrived at Iraklion in the late afternoon, we checked to see when the boat to Rhodes was leaving and found we'd have to take another bus to the other side of the island. The boat would leave at six o'clock the next morning. After a long day of more bus travel, we arrived at Ayios Nikolaos, very late at night. Cap suggested finding the youth hostel and taking a shower there and resting. Rest didn't come easily, though, since we found something to fight about the whole night.

At six the following morning, we boarded the boat for a horrible journey to Rhodes. We traveled deck class as usual; it stormed all the way, and the sea was terribly rough. Having already lost a night's sleep, we were dead tired. The boat was due to arrive in the early evening, but it didn't dock until after midnight. There were no bunks on this boat, so we tried sleeping on the wooden benches. That worked for a couple of hours, until we were discovered and kicked out. People were sick and throwing up everywhere. Suitcases, chairs, and people were being thrown all over the place. Finally, I went back downstairs to the staff quarters and searched for a place to stay. A very sympathetic crewmember thought I looked tired and offered me his bunk, an actual bed with a mattress. I just couldn't believe my good fortune; I hurried back upstairs and told Cap. We shut ourselves in the little room and finally rested. The chaos was so terrible where the rest of the passengers were that I spent the rest of the time in that room. My only venture outside was to go to the kitchen to buy some food from the staff. Food in Greece is normally delicious, but it is very greasy, covered with olive oil. This food seemed to be the oiliest I'd ever seen. One look at it and I decided to go hungry.

There were a few bright spots during that miserable boat trip, though. One stop along the way was at the island of Karpathos. The harbor there looked like something out of a fairy tale with its whitewashed buildings, mountains, and blue sea. It was very peaceful compared to the miserable scene on the boat.

We docked at Rhodes in the pouring rain. Cap and I found a taxi to take us to a hotel in the center of town. What luxury that clean, neat room seemed after our long boat trip. This luxurious room cost us about five dollars per night.

After a good night's sleep, we got up to find another lackluster day with pouring-down rain. Our first thought was how to escape the dreariness. It seemed we were always running, always searching for something better. Turkey was a possibility, we thought. Neither of us had ever been to Asia, so Turkey would be a new exploration for us both.

The mountains of Turkey were visible in the far distance from Rhodes. We found a travel agent who informed us that the only boat to Turkey left once a week; so, naturally, we made reservations to leave on it two days later. For the remainder of our time there, we explored the town of Rhodes, the Old City, and shops.

The next day, the weather was better, so we rented a motorcycle and rode to Lindos, a small town at the other end of the island. This was the kind of place and kind of weather we'd been searching for. The day was gorgeous, sunny, and comfortable. We stopped along the way at little coffee shops and had soft drinks. At the numerous roadside orchards, we picked oranges, stopping often to eat and just to enjoy the surrounding beauty.

We traveled through the countryside. Just at the top of the mountain at the far end of the island, we could see Lindos, white and gleaming in the sun below us. We spent the day roaming through the narrow streets, which were particularly quiet since no cars were allowed in town. We explored the town castle and sunned ourselves on the beach. Life seemed pretty good.

"This is just perfect," Cap told me, smiling and taking my hand as we strolled through the cobblestone streets of Lindos. "This is the kind of vacation we wanted."

"You're right," I replied, squeezing his hand. "It couldn't be better."

Yes, we were happy again. The urge for drugs seemed to have disappeared. The weather was good, and the countryside and villages were a paradise. Both of us had high expectations for the rest of the trip.

But unfortunately, those expectations would not materialize.

CHAPTER 3

February 21, 1970

*E*arly the next morning, Cap and I arrived at the dock and looked for our boat to Turkey. Where was it? All we could see in the harbor was a little rickety-looking fishing boat that was flying the red and white Turkish flag. That certainly didn't look like a boat that would cross the sea, we thought. A few other passengers headed for Turkey gathered around the immigration desk.

"We're going to Turkey," Cap said to a little old man dressed in black. "Do you know when the boat will arrive?"

The man pointed his finger at the fishing boat.

"No, I mean the boat that is going to Turkey," Cap protested.

Another passenger joined our group and informed us that the little fishing boat was indeed our boat. Not believing them, we went closer to inspect it.

The boat was about the size of a small cabin cruiser, unpainted and fragile-looking. I looked at Cap and he looked at me.

"Will this boat make it to Turkey?" Cap wondered aloud.

"Well, maybe if the water's calm." I stood there contemplating the night we'd spent on the huge boat to Crete. "I don't know. What should we do?"

We finally agreed that since we had been told that this was the boat and there appeared to be no other way to get to Turkey, we would go along with the plan. We boarded. After all, this boat must make the trip all the time.

Our crew was composed of rugged dark Turkish men with deeply lined faces. Their personalities seemed to match their looks. None of them was friendly. No one smiled.

Despite our initial worries, our trip ended up being spectacular. The weather had cleared up some and the sea was calm. Sitting outside on the deck, we watched Turkey grow closer and closer. When we neared the coast, we passed between mountains for a couple of hours to reach our destination, Marmaris. It was a very impressive journey.

However, as we neared the dock at Marmaris, our ideas began to change. The weather was overcast, the buildings near the port were gray, and the whole scene before us appeared ominous. There were groups of dark, sullen-looking men standing watching the boat come in. Those men certainly added to the impression of gloominess. All of their clothing was somber and dark colored. Their pants were ragged and their suit jackets mismatched. Most of them were wearing dark beret-style hats; all of them resembled the sinister-looking boat crew. They stared at us, even more so than the Greeks had stared at us in Athens.

Cap said, "My God, let's go back to Greece!"

I felt the same way. We both were paranoid.

But we were there and we weren't going back. We got off the boat and went through immigration and customs in a tiny little house by the dock. The crowds of men followed and watched our every move.

After making a search for someone who could speak a little English, we found a man and asked him where there was a hotel. The man pointed out a pension on the street facing the water. The room we were shown was fine, so we took it and went out to explore the town.

Almost immediately, a young Turkish man came up to us and spoke to us in English. This man was just the opposite of the men who had been on the pier. He had shoulder-length hair and was dressed in Western trendy dress. And what did he ask us?

"Do you want to buy some hash?"

At this question, Cap's eyes lit up. Here was a friend.

So we spent the rest of the afternoon with Ahmet—and some of his friends who joined us. We went for çay (tea) that was served in tiny hourglass-shaped glasses. We drank glasses and glasses of it at two cents a pop. The çay house was tiny, dark, and filled with men. So far I

21

hadn't seen a Turkish woman. And in fact, the entire time I was to stay in Marmaris, I would see only three. The feeling of being surrounded always by dark, mean-looking men was a very uncomfortable one, to say the least.

For most of the first afternoon in Marmaris, Cap and I sat in that shop drinking çay in the little curved glasses. Cap was excited, but impatient too, because Ahmet said he would be able to locate some hashish for us that night. The happiness he'd felt and shown the day we went to Lindos had disappeared. He had returned to his original behavior on the trip; nothing could have excited him more than hash.

Despite the constant presence of dark, scary-looking men, Marmaris was pretty, a gorgeous village. Surrounded on three sides by high mountains, it was at the end of a long twisting bay that led to the open sea, kilometers away. The houses and buildings in Marmaris had orange-tiled roofs and were constructed of a beige-gray stucco material instead of the whitewashed material the Greeks used.

Out of my ignorance, I had expected Turkey to be similar to Morocco, the only other Muslim country I'd visited. But no, the only resemblance to Morocco I'd observed so far was the mosques and the call to prayer from the minarets. The Turks didn't wear djellabas or robes. The three women I'd seen so far weren't veiled. I hadn't seen anyone praying in the streets. I was curious about the differences.

That night, we met Ahmet and some of his friends and then went to his house to smoke. I couldn't believe that anyone could live in that house, but it was just the first of many such houses I saw on that trip. To reach it, we walked through numerous tiny alleys in the dark unlighted streets. Finally, we came to a doorway and entered a miniscule room. There were seven of us crowded inside. The room was furnished with two small mattresses on the floor, a table the size of a TV table, and a woodstove. Our host was an old, dark, rough-looking man, typical of the Turks, I decided, but even rougher looking, if that was possible. Soon the room was filled with the smoke of joints the size of a Tampax. After my Icelandic experience, I faked smoking. There was no way I was going to get stoned in that claustrophobic room. Just being there was enough of a trip in itself. The host brewed çay, and again it was served in those little curved glasses.

After all the men were stoned to their satisfaction, we all left the tiny room and went in search of food. Ahmet suggested a restaurant where tables were set up outside in the freezing cold. He ordered *et sote* (sautéed meat stew) for all of us. Everyone ate from a communal plate in the center of the table. This was the first time I'd shared my food like this; I wasn't sure I wanted to eat. But with hunger overcoming my repulsion, I filled my stomach. The food was good—small pieces of beef sautéed with onions and mushrooms. It didn't take long for me to accept the practice of eating from the same bowl with other people. This was the Turkish way of eating. Soon it felt normal to me.

After the satisfying meal, Cap was in a mood to go to another çay shop. I was tired of running around and wanted to go back to the hotel. Quite an argument followed. Cap left and went to the çay shop with the others, while I returned to the hotel. Our romance was slowly, but surely, dying. We were fighting so much that I found myself wondering how I'd ever been attracted to him in the first place. I found myself more and more disgusted with him, his childishness, and his immaturity. I too was immature, but our values and aspirations were very different.

Our new Turkish friends planned a picnic for the following day. A group of ten picked us up, and then we all climbed a small mountain at the edge of town. The Turks had prepared lots of good food and brought enough wine for everyone. Ahmet told Cap about his planned job for the coming summer, diving for sponges and dynamiting fish illegally. Ahmet was encouraging Cap and me to participate. Cap got quite excited about the prospect. I wasn't so sure. We had return tickets to the States that had to be used by the end of April. Would we have enough money to stay and then buy other tickets later? We were doing well financially so far, but staying that much longer would be stretching things a bit, in my opinion. Besides, I was planning on traveling to the rest of the Mediterranean area, especially Lebanon and Egypt. Still, a summer on the sea on a Turkish boat didn't sound too bad. But then there was the other question: dynamiting fish illegally? What if we decided to stay and then got caught?

I spent time that day talking to one of the Turks who was a college student in Istanbul. He was different from the rest, seeming to have a serious plan for his life, instead of just fooling around in Marmaris like the others. It was a relief to get to know someone who wasn't always thinking of drugs and other illegal things.

My and Cap's next planned move was to Istanbul, mainly because it was the Turkish city we knew of. It just seemed the natural thing to travel there. The next day, a bus was leaving for Izmir, the town where one changes buses for Istanbul. The bus ride took all day and went through beautiful mountainous countryside. We enjoyed seeing the picturesque people and villages along the way. It was a peaceful ride—no fighting for a change.

In the late afternoon, we arrived in Izmir and decided to stay overnight, since we didn't know when buses left for Istanbul. After inquiring at several hotels, we settled on one. Cap was very upset that the price was a bit higher than we'd paid before in other places. Still, I said it didn't matter; the important thing was to find a place to rest.

The first thing Cap wanted to do was to have a hot shower. We didn't have a bathroom in our room. When he tried to take a shower in the hall bathroom, the water was frigid.

Wrapped in a towel, he strode down to the front desk to ask the hotel owner for a hot shower.

"I need a hot shower—now," he yelled, gesturing wildly.

The hotel owner looked at him and responded in Turkish.

"I can't understand you, you idiot," Cap screamed. "I want a hot shower."

After much heated monologue from Cap in English, the owner finally understood what Cap wanted. He gestured that Cap would have to wait while the water was heated.

Cap yelled, "Fuck you. I don't want to wait."

This scene was without a doubt the most embarrassing thing I'd seen Cap do so far in a foreign country. Why couldn't I just sink through the floor? I'd heard Cap swear at his mother and friends before, which was bad enough, but I'd never heard him do it in public with a stranger. In his rage, Cap decided he wanted to go to Istanbul immediately. He ordered me out to find the bus station and to ask for the next bus leaving. I gladly left him there—anything to keep him quiet and to let me escape the scene.

But I couldn't find the bus station. Of course, I didn't yet know a word of Turkish. There I was in a strange country at night in the middle of a city, not knowing where to look. Knowing that we'd come in on the bus, I tried to find my way back to that station. Then I entered a shop and asked if someone spoke English. No one did. As I walked, I tried to remember where I was going so I'd be able to return to the hotel. Finally, I found a little old man who understood the words *bus* and *station*. These words are actually quite similar to the Turkish—respectively *otobüs* and *istasyon*. He directed me to a little office, where I tried to ask the people when the next bus left for Istanbul. I left with a list of times but never did find out whether or not they were correct.

Somehow I made it back to the hotel thinking that it was amazing what I could do if I had to get something specific accomplished. Cap had recovered his sanity and was in an apologetic mood since he had had his shower and had dressed up for the evening. He suggested going out for a nice dinner to make up.

And we did just that.

After dinner, we decided to take a walk. I wished we never had. We found a little district with very narrow crowded streets. Several boys came up to us and offered to sell us hashish.

I warned Cap not to buy any, even though he wanted to.

"How do we know we can trust them? We don't want to get into trouble here."

He agreed with me, amazingly enough, and turned them away.

But pretty soon, a more hip-looking guy came up and tried to speak to Cap in Turkish. Somehow the vibes were right this time—or Cap felt they were—and he agreed to enter a taxi with this guy. I didn't want to go with them, but I was also afraid to be left behind. And I wasn't sure what was going on either. We got into the taxi, along with two other Turks, plus the driver. Cap, one Turk, and I were in the backseat. There seemed to be no meter in the taxi; I was worried about paying a huge bill. None of the Turks spoke English; no sign language was used.

Soon, a tampon-sized joint was rolled and passed around the car. Hash was also passed around to eat. I didn't want to smoke, but I did eat some hash, convinced it would do nothing to me. I was wrong. I started feeling as if I were in a dream. And as Cap became more and more stoned, my fear increased as the taxi went farther and farther into the dark countryside.

And I was right to be frightened. Suddenly, the car stopped. The driver demanded three hundred lira. This we could understand. Lira was money, and the three hundred was made quite clear in sign language. That meant twenty-five dollars. I knew I had been right to worry about what we were doing. Cap seemed nearly ready to pass out, so I tried to explain to the Turks that our money was in our hotel, hoping they'd drive us back there to get it—and then we could escape. But they refused to understand as I continued to try to tell them we had no money with us.

"*Otel—yok* lira" (Hotel—no lira), I kept saying.

Frustrated with me, they finally started the taxi and began slowly driving toward town. Occasionally, they'd stop and continue demanding the money. I was panicked, unable to understand why Cap wasn't saying anything to help me.

And it was true that Cap was being unlike himself, very quiet. Then suddenly he began to throw up into the far corner of the car, all over the guy beside him. The poor guy threw open the door, ran away, and didn't return. Despite the fact that I was by now completely grossed out, maybe Cap's vomiting was a blessing in disguise, because obviously the Turks were disgusted too and started driving faster toward town. They asked the name of our hotel. I couldn't remember it, but somehow (who knows how?) I directed them to the spot. Cap sat gloomily beside me. I felt too revolted for words.

When we stopped in front of the hotel, Cap jumped out of the taxi and ran inside. I told the Turks that I would go to the room and then return with the money they wanted. As I entered the hotel, Cap appeared with the manager, who helped him clean the vomit from his clothes. Then the manager went outside and talked to the Turks, who disappeared fast. I was surprised that the manager would do anything for Cap to help him after the fit Cap had thrown that afternoon over the hot shower.

We returned to our room. I could think of nothing to say to Cap; I was speechless with fury. His stupidity, his grossness, his irresponsibility! Since I was too disgusted with him to tell him my feelings coherently,

I was silent. Maybe that was the best thing, because he knew I was upset and apologized. He did feel that at least the sickness had gotten us out of the situation (implying that he had planned to vomit). No matter what he said, though, I felt that nothing was going to turn me on to him again. I was finished with him.

Sure, I was finished with Cap, I thought. But breaking up with him wasn't going to be easy. Under no circumstances did I want to return to the United States early. Doing that would be worse than traveling with Cap. And also, I certainly wasn't going to travel alone in Turkey. So my thoughts ended there.

Later that night, Cap decided to throw up again. Instead of going across the hall to the toilet, he just leaned over the edge of the bed and covered the floor with the stuff. I left the room wondering how and why I had ever gotten involved with him in the first place. It was just too much for me. To top off everything, I had to tell him to clean up his mess, as he was going to leave it for the maid in the morning. He actually expected us to sleep in the same room with that puke.

In the morning, we packed our bags and set out to look for the bus to Istanbul. Izmir was a place hated by both of us now, through no fault of its own. It was pouring rain and cold out. We had no luck finding the bus station or any information. Someone advised us to take a taxi to a certain address. We climbed into a horse-drawn carriage and were overcharged for the ride. There was nothing we could do about that. And then there was no station at the address that had been given to us. Cap started getting into one of his tantrum moods again. I felt helpless and didn't know what to do.

Finally, I thought of an idea. We could find a high-class hotel. Maybe someone there would speak English and be able to answer our questions. Since there was an expensive hotel in the area we were in, we walked to it. And it turned out that my idea was a good one, even though Cap was still furious and approached the desk clerk in a temper. He treated him as if the whole thing in Izmir was this guy's fault. I wanted to sink through the floor in embarrassment. After ordering Cap to sit down, I talked to the clerk myself. Fortunately he spoke fluent English. I explained our problem. The man was great; he told us the bus schedule and said that since the bus had left already for

Istanbul that day, we could stay in his place until the next day. Then he took us there.

The man, Mustafa, had a nice apartment, fairly modern with a kitchen, a bathroom, and two bedrooms. He showed us around and then went back to the hotel to finish his day's work. We were relieved. Looking back on it, though, I wonder why we were so trusting this time after all we'd been through. We cleaned up, dried off, and rested.

When Mustafa came home, we had dinner, something he'd brought in for us, and then talked. He had been educated in Greece and had been in England for a while. He was convinced that we shouldn't go on to Istanbul, saying that instead we should look for a quiet, warm place, since that's what we'd originally come overseas for. He knew of a little village on the south coast of Turkey that he loved, Side (pronounced "See-day"), and which he highly recommended. He usually spent his vacations in Side, he said. The problem was that the bus for Side left only twice a week and we'd have to wait two days to get it. But we were welcome to stay in his apartment as long as we liked.

Mustafa had sold us on Side. His place was very comfortable and free. And he was very nice. Given these things, we decided to wait for the bus.

The next couple of days were fun. Mustafa's friends stopped by and we had good discussions. One night we went to see a friend of his, a US Army officer. We listened to rock records and talked and drank. Usually Mustafa went out in the pouring rain and bought food back for us all to eat—hot kebabs, vegetable stews, raw vegetables, pilaf, all really delicious. And because of Mustafa, who didn't smoke, we had no hash. Happily for me, Cap didn't seem to mind.

And my questions about Turkish-Muslim dress were answered. Mustafa just happened to have a Turkish history book in English. I read that Turkey's first president, Mustafa Kemal Atatürk, proposed a series of laws in 1925 progressively limiting certain items of traditional clothing. And in 1934, another law was passed banning the wearing of religion-based clothing, such as the veil and turban, while actively promoting Western-style attire.

When the day came to leave, Cap and I boarded the bus for Antalya, the closest town to Side. Again, it was an interesting bus ride. We even saw a camel caravan along the way. Turkey was becoming more and more exotic to us. The ride took about twelve hours. The days I'd spent at Mustafa's had been good with Cap again. Somehow, it seemed he'd returned to being the old Cap with whom I'd fallen in love. Despite some doubts, my hopes returned.

In the late afternoon, we arrived at Antalya. Mustafa had instructed us how to get to Side—by first finding a *dolmuş* (shared taxi). This was confusing since we didn't know where to look and, as usual, couldn't make ourselves understood easily, but we finally located the place for the *dolmuş*. A young Turkish guy said he'd drive us to Side for ninety lira (about seven dollars). This was almost as much as the bus ride from Izmir had cost. We knew we were being grossly overcharged. We found out later that the correct fare should have been about one dollar. But we didn't know anything at the time, which fact was obvious to the Turks. So we climbed into the *dolmuş* and headed for Side by way of Manavgat. According to our map, Manavgat was out of the way, a town on the other side of Side. We tried to complain, and the others tried to explain what was happening, but as usual, we didn't understand. Soon, we saw that the driver had to first drop off some other passengers.

Finally, we pulled up to some old Roman ruins. The driver said, "Side." *What is that?* I wondered. It certainly wasn't a little fishing village. We protested and said, "*Otel.*" They obliged by driving farther, finally pulling up at a motel.

By now, it was dark and it was hard to see anything in the unlighted village. The hotel owner came outside and then carried our bags in for us. His name was Berker, a well-dressed man in his early thirties. He spoke English pretty well. Berker showed us to our room, which was inexpensive, we thought at that time—$2.50. The room was cold; he supplied an electric heater. We had a bathroom with a Western toilet (we found out later that this was highly unusual in the village—an Asian toilet was a very different thing). Our room looked out onto the sea, which was a few meters away. Berker invited us to the dining room for dinner. We ate with him and his little nephew who was visiting from Crete and who spoke very good English. Berker told us that many of the people in Side originally came from Crete and spoke Greek and

Turkish. The meal we had was fantastic. And Berker kept ordering and ordering. I especially loved the soup.

Cap and I were really pleased with the place we'd found. Here we felt like we were living in luxury after what we'd been through. From what we could see in the dark, it was great to live right on the sea. The people so far were nice, and the food was wonderful. And we thought everything was very inexpensive.

In the hotel lobby, I found a brochure in English explaining Side's known history. It began with the Greeks who escaped from Troy after its fall. After that, a series of peoples inhabited it, starting with the Seleucids of Syria and the Ptolemies of Egypt, and ending in the tenth century with the Romans. After Side was abandoned in the tenth century, it was eventually resettled when a group of fishermen migrated from Crete in the early twentieth century.

The village is on a peninsula and Roman ruins, the high point of which is the theater, which surrounds the village. Two long beaches stretch away from the village on the east and the west. Our motel was on the eastern beach away from the village a bit. It was a beautiful location.

Our time in Side began well enough. The first day, we took a walk through the Roman ruins and came upon some gypsies camped in a tent. The floor of the tent was covered with animal skins and handwoven blankets. The gypsies invited us in and tried to sell us Roman coins they'd found. Cap was tempted and finally bought a couple. I thought this was ridiculous since I felt the coins couldn't possibly be real anyway. I still don't know if I was right or wrong about that. But it was an interesting experience. And the family was really warm and friendly too—especially after we'd bought the coins.

One morning we went into town to have breakfast, instead of having the huge one offered at the motel. There were three restaurants in the village center, all right on the sea. We ordered a Turkish breakfast and received Feta cheese, olives, bread, and of course çay. While we were there, a very handsome Turkish man came up to us and invited us to a party that night in the village. Cap told him maybe. It was obvious to me that he wasn't interested. The young Turk was Süleyman, who would turn out to be very important in the days to come. Süleyman told me later that he could never figure out why we hadn't shown up at the party that night.

I have neglected to mention until now that most of the young Turkish men in Side spoke at least some English. They'd learned it from the young tourists like us who'd started invading Side a few years prior. The village was still unspoiled, as rich people and older tourists hadn't discovered it yet. On top of that, the few of them who were brought in by tour bus to see the Roman ruins wouldn't have been happy with the accommodations that we were happy to accept.

Even though we both liked Side, Cap and I were still having problems. We would fight and argue about our ideas and what we should do. Finally, Cap decided (and I was glad of it) that we should spend more time away from each other. One day, he told me he wanted to go into the village and search for the foreign freaks he'd spied on a walk. I was happy about this, because it was a nice day and I wanted to lie in the sun. So he took off. Later in the day when the sun had disappeared, I decided to walk to the village too. Unfortunately for me, another young Turkish guy, Hassan, whom we'd met earlier, saw me and bothered me for the rest of the afternoon. He followed me everywhere and kept trying to kiss me and touch me. I kept trying to turn him off by saying I loved Cap; he didn't believe me and said that he could tell by watching me when I was with Cap that I didn't love him at all. This was very perceptive of him, I thought. So we kept wandering around the ruins by the sea. Finally I got sick of the whole thing and went back to the room

Meanwhile that same day, Cap met his freaks. There was a Danish couple, Gry and Clemens; an Italian guy, Rusty; a French woman, Danielle; and a Mexican woman, Gloria. Cap was very excited, saying that they were "great people" and that they wanted to start a commune in Side. He really wanted to get in on that and simply stay in Side indefinitely. I wasn't excited at all about his idea, instead wanting to get on with our traveling and see more of the Middle East. But Cap convinced me to go into town with him that night and meet his new friends. He'd also met some Turks who made jewelry. He was planning to begin working with them.

We'd previously promised Berker that he could take us to his discotheque in the village that night. I felt funny refusing after we'd agreed, so Cap finally consented to go, saying we'd slip out later and join the others. Cap was right; the discotheque was boring. No one was there but us. The club itself was tiny and nicely decorated with small tables and stools, fishnet, and Turkish baskets. We were sitting there with Berker, bored, when in walked the freaks, much to Cap's happiness. They invited us to their pension and off we went, along with Berker, who wasn't too happy about it. He left soon afterward. Of course, everyone was smoking huge joints brought from Pakistan by two Arabs, Mohammed and Arafat.

Gry, a beautiful blonde Danish woman, told Cap and me that we were paying much too much for our room in the motel. She told us that she and Clemens only paid seventy cents for their room and that there was a vacancy in that place. Upon hearing this, Cap became very excited about moving. Even I didn't mind the idea. I hadn't realized how inexpensive Turkey could be. So we talked to the owner of the pension, Ali. Ali was a tall Turk who face was deeply scarred. Ali said we could move into the pension in a couple of days.

That night, my and Cap's walk back to the motel was spooky. Electricity in Side goes off at eleven at night, so the whole road was black. We could make out the ruins along the side of the road. Everything looked eerie, particularly so because we were both stoned (yes, I had decided to try smoking once again).

Meanwhile, Hassan had been watching me. I knew he was up to something. One day when I was lying on our terrace in the sun, he approached me. *Ugh! These Turks,* I thought. I told Hassan that I was Cap's girl and that he should leave me alone. It seemed to be difficult to convince these guys of that, but finally Hassan left, not too happy.

Cap's new friend, Tarik, and his family owned one of the nicest hotels in town. Cap and I often went there because we liked Tarik's place. It was on the sea and had a big glassed-in porch. This is where everyone sat and drank çay, read, talked, and made jewelry—a general meeting place for tourists and young Turkish men. Tarik had a brother, Cem, who was quite friendly and had lots of books in English. The books and the general conversation kept me interested. I was told that Tarik' father's photo had been published in *National Geographic* years ago. And Cap, through Tarik, had discovered a new interest—making jewelry. Cap and Tarik were working with copper wire and evil-eye beads (a beautiful blue and white glass bead resembling an eye). Their designs were really nice. I asked Tarik if he'd make me an evil-eye necklace, and he said he'd be glad to. Later he gave it to me as a gift, but I insisted on paying him $1.50 for the beautiful handmade beaded necklace.

February 28, 1970
Side, Turkey

Dear Family,

I've finally decided to buy an air letter. It's easier, and I can say more than I can on a postcard. I feel badly about not having written much before. We've been on the move, and as usual it's hard finding post offices when you want them.

I last wrote from Rhodes, I think. Since then, we came to Turkey on a small fishing boat with ten other passengers. We landed in a small village, Marmaris, and stayed there a day. Some Turkish men we met showed us around and took us on a picnic in the mountains. We then spent a long day on a bus for Izmir.

Turkey is mountainous, rocky, and less developed than any place I've been before. Izmir was unbelievable. We had to stop there for connections to Istanbul. However, a series of bad experiences (in detail when I see you) changed our minds, and we decided to go south instead. We stayed two nights at a Turkish man's place.

Now we're in Side, a tiny village in southern Turkey on the sea. There are some beautiful Roman ruins here, and we're staying in the town's "expensive" motel for about $2.50/night with breakfast. Balcony and windows are right on the beach. But we're having rainy weather. You can't have everything, I guess.

Cap and a Turkish friend are making jewelry from copper wire today. I decided it was high time I wrote you a decent letter. The lack of news from me does not mean I'm not thinking of you—because I do, a lot.

We have enough money left to stay a while at these prices. But if we get itchy again and move, of course, that will shorten our stay. I'd still like to see Cyprus, Lebanon, and Egypt if possible. Transportation out of here will be a problem. We had to rent a minibus to get us to Side from the last big town.

Turkish food has been the best so far. The food in Greece was really greasy and oily.

I wish it would warm up again. The surf is beautiful, but it's too chilly to swim, and I've lost my tan from Matala.

Yesterday Cap and I were wandering through the ruins and found a nomad goatherd's tent. The grandmother, I think, the parents, and two kids were there, and invited us in their tent to look at Roman and other coins they'd found. We finally bought some. They say it's easy to find coins around here on your own.

Cap has been offered a job on a sponge boat here for the summer, and I think he will probably come over and stay after that to make jewelry. I expect we'll probably get back to the States sometime in March, but I'll let you know what's happening before then.

I'd love to write so many things in detail, but I know they'd be better told in person. Cap has been taking movies, and I'm really getting anxious to see how they're coming out.

I'll go for now and will try to be better about writing from now on.

Love to all of you,
Karen

Two nights before we were to move into the pension, it was pouring rain. Cap and I were in the village with Rusty, the Italian. Rusty was a skinny little guy, weirdly dressed in filthy suede pants. His hair was a flowing mess of tight curls. He was particularly odd compared to the other freaks; he had no money and relied on others to give him food. And he slept out in the ruins.

Cap, deciding he felt sorry for him, offered to let him sleep in our room on that rainy night. I wasn't comfortable with the idea and wasn't sure why, but since it was pouring, there was nothing I felt I could do to talk him out of it. So along came Rusty. There was only one double bed in the room and no soft chairs.

Cap said, "Well, we'll all sleep together."

This was too much for me, but it was quite late and I didn't know what else I could do. When we got ready for bed, I left on my underwear and got in on the edge of the bed, opposite Rusty, hoping Cap would take the middle. But Cap was in one of his obnoxious and thoughtless moods, as usual.

"Get in the middle," he insisted.

Completely disgusted, but not wanting to appear as if I didn't trust Rusty, who was pretending to sleep, I finally moved over, trying to squish onto Cap's side.

For a while, all was quiet. But then, it began—Rusty's hands. He really attacked me with his almost painful caresses. I tried to get away and told Cap what Rusty was doing.

"C'mon, Cap. He's touching me and hurting me," I complained.

"Karen, you're just being square," Cap replied.

"Calm down. Cap's right," Rusty agreed, accusing me of being hysterical and being a stupid American woman.

Rusty was right in one way: I was definitely becoming hysterical. I didn't know what to do other than to yell at Rusty to leave me alone. Mostly, however, I was shocked beyond words at Cap; I knew he was messed up, but I'd thought he had some feelings for me anyway. He'd shown jealousy many times in the past. But Rusty and Cap had both been drinking heavily that night. Nothing could stop their little game at my expense. When I insulted Rusty enough, he quit trying to touch me. And then Cap got the brilliant idea of trying to make love to me right there in front of Rusty. This was too much for me. I turned on my stomach and swore at him.

Unbelievably, they both left me alone after that.

The next morning, Rusty got up and left early without speaking to either of us. I got up and went to have breakfast alone, not knowing what I was going to do. What a hellish nightmare I was living. I couldn't figure out how I had ever gotten into this situation. Finally, Cap got up and sheepishly approached me. He actually apologized before I had a chance to say a thing. For him to be ashamed of anything was unreal. At the time, I felt there wasn't much else I could do but accept the apology and go on. I knew the trip couldn't last much longer. So we went ahead and celebrated his birthday, which happened to be that very day.

I had previously made arrangements with the cook in the motel to bake Cap a cake, since I couldn't think of anything else to get him for his birthday. The cake turned out beautifully, and the meal was fantastic as usual. But now that we were going to leave the motel, we started wondering just what the meals were going to cost us. We'd been stupid and naïve to assume they'd be inexpensive just like everything else. And we'd been idiots never to ask Berker. Luckily for us, they were low-priced, although they did cost a lot more than we would have spent if we'd eaten in the village.

The birthday was celebrated as I'd planned. We had dinner with candlelight by the sea. Photos of us could have been published in a travel magazine—the perfect romantic vacation. We professed our love for each other and our hopes for the future. It's possible that Cap meant what he said, but I know I didn't. I had given up hope.

CHAPTER 4

In a few days, Cap and I moved into Ali's pension, which was a two-story house. Ali and his family lived downstairs, and there were four rooms for tourists upstairs, all bordering on a long concrete balcony and facing the sea. There was a little gas burner on the balcony where everyone cooked commune style. Also, there was an outdoor sink for all of us and a little Eastern-style toilet, the kind that is found many places in Asia and Africa. Footprints are molded on the concrete floor with a hole between them. One is supposed to put one's feet into the footprints, relieve oneself into the hole, and then use water from a bucket for washing hands and flushing.

The other people in the pension were Clemens and Gry, the Danes, both with their long blond curly flyaway hair. Then there were Mohammed and Arafat, the Arabs, and Danielle, the Frenchwoman. Gloria, the Mexican, lived downstairs. Of course Rusty was around a lot, always hoping for a handout.

Things really started getting terrible with Cap once we'd moved into the pension. The Arabs had lots of hash that they had brought from Pakistan and were taking to Germany to sell to the US troops. So hash was everywhere. Cap spent quite a bit of money on some and expected to carry it back to the States and sell it. He was always discussing the best way of hiding the hash in order to cross borders. The most popular idea was to insert it into the sole of a shoe. Thinking that would be an extraordinarily dangerous thing to do, I violently disagreed with the idea. I didn't have any urge to trying to transport hash with me by any means, even though I had finally overcome my fear of smoking and was doing a lot of it by then. It seemed that there was always a joint being passed around. I almost got to the point that I wasn't even aware of being stoned, because I was so used to it.

Usually Danielle cooked our meals. Even though I was now used to eating communal style with the Turks, it turned me off to eat out of one big pot with this particular group of people. Danielle, in particular, was really filthy. But I gradually got accustomed to this eating style too. And it was cheaper than eating in the restaurants. So I joined them.

One rainy day, Cap, Danielle, and I went to Antalya because we wanted to see a Turkish bath. Actually, the baths were closed that day, but those two finally convinced the owner to open them up for us. Cap went into the men's side and Danielle and I into the women's. I wasn't impressed. The place was all concrete, including the seats and benches, and there was running hot water. I suppose if one didn't have a normal place to bathe (as we didn't), it was fine, but it wasn't very pleasant. It was fun, though, to be in the large town of Antalya after having been in the small village. Later, we filled up on baklava, which wasn't sold in Side regularly.

One of the constant preoccupations around the pension was with music. The Arabs were traveling with a recorder and a couple of drums. Everyone in the pension (except for me) felt that if you just sat there and made noise (not in relation to the other noises at all), it was great. This went on all the time, and it finally got to me. Even when I was stoned, the noise was hard to take, especially when I could see the players were all impressed with what they were doing. Cap was the ringleader, or at least probably the most enthusiastic participant in the music making. He constantly criticized me for just sitting there and listening.

"Why don't you do something? Don't just sit there," he would complain, with a disapproving look on his face.

I kept throwing his theory up to him. "It's beautiful if you do just what you feel. Those are your words. That's what you tell me all the time," I would reply. "And now you're saying I shouldn't just relax and listen. That's what I feel like doing. Just what is right anyway?"

But I knew the answer already. "Just what you feel" meant to him and the others just what *they* thought you should do. If you didn't conform to what they wanted, you were considered weird.

Cap also criticized me a lot for "not having a project." He was making his jewelry and I wasn't "being creative," he would say. I told him I could be creative if and when I wanted, but I didn't "feel like it" at that time. I was enjoying myself just relaxing. I am a voracious reader, but what books were around there for me to read? By this time, sick of defending myself, I was wondering even more just what I was doing there—and with him.

Berker appeared at the pension one day and demanded the money we owed him. He had finally made up our bill for the birthday dinner, charging us seven dollars for the birthday cake alone. Cap and I were both upset. By now, we had gotten the idea that living in Turkey could be very inexpensive and that we'd been overcharged a lot. Here Berker was trying to take us again. I was sure that you could buy a cake in America for dollars, and so a cake in Turkey should be far less. Cap argued with him and finally paid the bill. What else could we do? If I had known, I wouldn't have ordered the cake. I was finally learning that I had to check prices and then bargain in the Middle East.

So many things were dragging me down. My relationship with Cap was getting worse and worse, more and more frustrating. And the others in the pension weren't helping much. While depressed about my problems one day, I wrote to Dick, feeling he was at least someone I'd always been able to talk to. Being with Cap made the life I'd had with Dick look pretty good after all—despite my being in the gorgeous setting of Side. Sometimes, I felt like I'd made a huge mistake by leaving Dick.

Yes, Dick was a nice man. And each and every one of my previous boyfriends had been nice as well.

How on earth did I get involved with someone like Cap? I asked myself. The answer to that question was that traveling had brought out a nasty side of Cap's character that I hadn't seen in Washington. And I continued to believe I had to stick with him until our trip was over.

Most of the days were spent on the beach, which was a magnificent one, seeming to stretch on forever. Tall dunes ran along the beach, and the Roman ruins were behind them. Actually, there were two beach areas—our old motel beach area and the one on our side of the village, the latter being the one we used most. Since we all spent so much time on the beach, there were many "interesting" beach incidents.

Lots of the Turkish village boys came to the beach just to observe the foreigners. They just sat behind us on the dunes and stared. One time we caught one masturbating while he watched. We were a huge curiosity to them, especially when Gry decided to go topless, or when some of our companions skinny-dipped. I felt that it was bad enough to wear a bikini there, which I did because I didn't have any choice. Bikinis or any swimsuits were shocking enough to the Turks, who were used to seeing women bundled up in layers of clothing, but to strip naked was really crude in Turkey. However, being nude went along with the freak ideals. One couldn't talk them out of it. No one else seemed to care what I did, but Cap kept nagging me about not taking off my top.

One day the waves were especially huge. I decided to swim. Fearless as I was, having been a Red Cross lifeguard teacher, I swam straight out to sea through the waves. Then when I decided to turn around and head back, the waves started breaking over me and the undertow pulled me farther out to sea. At first, I assumed I could make it back to shore, but then I was pounded under the water a couple of times by the waves, which knocked the breath out of me. One of my legs felt cramped. Then terror set in. Now I knew why the Red Cross teaches that panic is the first cause of drowning. As I struggled to stay up, continuing to be knocked down by the waves, I tried to call to Cap and the others on shore. Luckily, they saw or heard me, and Cap and Clemens came running naked into the water. They made it about three-quarters of the way to me, and then they, too, started having trouble. But they talked to me, saying I could make it. I kept struggling to swim in. At long last, we all made it to the beach, where we collapsed. Somehow just their being near and talking to me had given me strength and courage—and they agreed with me that the sea was really dangerous that day. Ever since that time, I (who before had never been afraid of any waves) have been nervous about going into the sea when it is even a little bit rough. I no longer do it.

One day, Gry, Clemens, Cap, and I were sunning ourselves on the sand. Only Clemens was nude. Watching us and gradually moving closer and closer were several teenaged Turkish boys. They started teasing

Clemens and laughing at him. After about ten minutes of putting up with this mockery, Clemens lost his patience. He got up and tried to chase the boys away. This started a fight, one that, I have to say, was hilarious. Clemens with his straggly long blond hair looked like some sort of crazy naked caveman. No wonder the boys were laughing. The whole thing was really ridiculous. Eventually with Cap and Rusty's help, the boys were chased away.

Another day at the beach, several people were nude as usual, or partially so. And also as usual, some Turkish boys were staring at us from the top of a dune. Gradually, they moved down. Soon they were just a few feet away and wildly staring.

"Well, let's give them something to really stare at," Danielle said.

She was dressed in street clothes, but she suddenly stood up and began to slowly strip down. The boys' eyes nearly bulged out of their heads. And Danielle had told me I shouldn't wear a minidress into Antalya because it would offend the people! What was she doing?

Another group down the beach had observed this little display. Süleyman, the Turk who had invited us to a party the second day in Side, was there with a couple of tourists. This group was watching everything that happened. I could see how disgusted they were. Süleyman motioned me over and told me that Danielle should stop, saying that the Turks wouldn't understand what Danielle was doing or why. I agreed and said I'd do what I could, which was nothing, of course, as none of them would listen to me. Everyone except me in my group felt that the whole thing was very funny and that the Turks deserved it. I felt it was so offensive that I left and stood away from the group while Danielle continued her act.

Then Süleyman motioned me over again. I could see that he was quite interested in me. Yet he was certainly subtler in his approach than the other Turks had been. I found myself enjoying his company. He invited me to stay with his group on the beach. That suited me fine. I went and told Cap that I was going to sit with Süleyman and his friends. That suited him fine too.

Süleyman was just a little taller than I, muscular and slender, and had a gorgeous head of wavy brown hair and long sideburns. He was lighter-skinned than most Turks, though still very suntanned, with the typical rugged lined face. But he was good-looking and he appealed to me, especially his adorable smile. He spoke very broken English, but he was still able to communicate. Süleyman told me he'd learned English from tourists and that he could neither read nor write the language.

I spent an enjoyable afternoon with Süleyman and his English friends. Right before I left with my original group, he asked me to a party that night at the restaurant. I told him that I couldn't go, that I was traveling with Cap, who wouldn't be too pleased if I went to a party without him. Süleyman said that he knew I wasn't like the other "hippies." He also told me that he knew I didn't like Cap anymore.

"You not hippie," he said, shaking his head. "I know you not like Cap anymore. Come on."

"Please understand," I answered, explaining that I just couldn't get away that night.

Disappointed, I returned to the pension.

The next day, Süleyman was on the beach again—and so were Cap and I. Süleyman came up to me while Cap was in the water and tried again to persuade me to meet him that night at the restaurant. I knew better, but Süleyman's appeal was winning me over. This time, I decided I'd try.

And I did, but it was easier said than done. Cap, after seeing Süleyman and me talking that afternoon, suspected something and had decided to keep a closer watch on me. Every time I started to leave the pension, he would come up to me and start talking. Finally, I tried to leave to tell Süleyman I'd be late. This time, I got away, but Rusty came trailing behind. Rusty said he wanted to apologize about the night in the motel when he had tried to have sex with me. I hadn't spoken to him since that night, but still, he wanted to get something going between us, he said. I was very turned off and couldn't seem to get rid of him. So, giving up on getting to the restaurant alone, I decided to head back to the pension. It would be better than having Rusty follow me.

But on the way back, I met up with Cap, Gry, Clemens, and the rest of the group. They were headed for the grocery store to buy dinner. Cap was upset with me and wondered why I'd wandered off (strange, since he would have been pleased a few days earlier if I'd exhibited "such independence"). Finally, I decided that if Süleyman had invited me to a real party, I'd tell Cap about it and we'd all go; then maybe I could get to be alone with Süleyman and tell him what had happened.

This worked beautifully; all of us showed up at the restaurant, much to Süleyman's surprise. People were singing and dancing. Cap decided to drink—on top of being stoned. I went over to Süleyman's table and sat with him. Cap, in his mood, didn't take too much notice of that. The evening went on. Quite a bit later, Süleyman suggested he and I leave and go to another party. I looked over at Cap and saw he wasn't paying any attention, so out I walked with Süleyman, feeling very daring. But what the hell! I was only with Cap now because I didn't know what else to do. Leave and travel alone? Go "home"? These questions erased any guilty feelings I may have had when leaving with Süleyman.

Süleyman took me to an upstairs room in a pension, his father's, as it turned out. An American man, Damon, had been living there for a few months. The place was great; there was a fireplace, comfortable colorful couches, and bright striped rugs on the floor. A different group of people were there. I recognized lots of them as Turks I'd seen and other tourists. This was a quieter group, not "hippies," older people who had something interesting to talk about. These were Süleyman's friends. I liked them. We sat around and talked and listened to music. A couple of people asked me about Cap. Why was I with him? Why did I stay with him? I tried to explain that right now I didn't know what else to do, but I certainly was going to get out of the relationship as soon as I could.

When Süleyman and I left that party, he took me through the dark narrow lanes to a tiny house. The wooden structure was one very small room. Inside this room there was only space enough for one single bed, a wood-burning heater, a gas burner for cooking, and a tiny table. There was only about a meter between the bed and the wall. A window looked out over the attached greenhouse. This house belonged to Muharrem, a very handsome Turk who had been at the pension party. Süleyman told me that Muharrem had built this house by himself.

Obviously, Muharrem and Süleyman had arranged that Süleyman would take me to Muharrem's place. Süleyman did turn out to be the typical fast mover, but he did have some cool. I found myself really liking him and becoming increasingly turned on by him. I had no ideas about what would happen after this night, but I decided to live day by day. Meanwhile, why not enjoy myself? Which is just what I did.

When I returned to the pension much later that night, Cap was in bed and decided to be very romantic. He had the feeling that something was going on and maybe he was going to lose me—at least, that was how he was acting. He made no accusations, but his bad moods and his taking me for granted had stopped. But it was too late and had been for a long time. He really made me sick! I pretended to sleep.

The next day, I again saw Süleyman for a short time on the beach. He suggested meeting again that night. I told him I couldn't, saying that Cap and I were invited to a party. I couldn't tell him the location because I didn't know it myself.

The party was in the ruins; actually it must have been in the basement of a ruined building. It took us quite some time to find it. When we did, we had to go through some narrow passages and then down some steps into a dungeon-like place. It was eerie and unreal. All the foreign freaks were there, along with several Turks. Some of them were playing their flutes and others were beating drums. Candles were lit. The whole thing was really dreamlike. Sitting on the stone floor, we drank in the atmosphere.

And then in walked Süleyman. I have to admit I was glad to see him. He had found the party, which wasn't very surprising in such a small village of six hundred people. The grapevine was extensive there; everyone knew what is going on everywhere, it seemed. Cap was sitting beside me, though, so I didn't feel I should pay much attention to Süleyman. Everyone was smoking. Soon Cap drifted to the other side of the room to play some music.

Süleyman came to sit beside me. He said, "Come. You and I leave."

"I can't," I whispered, shaking my head. "It's too dangerous."

He insisted, "Come on."

After thinking about my choices, I decided to change my mind. Cap wasn't looking anyway, and in fact, no one was paying any attention to us, so I got up and left with Süleyman. It was sort of a frightening thing to do, but I felt daring. And afterward was glad I had left. We took a long walk on the beach and to the theater. I returned home after Cap did. He was sleeping.

As I got ready for bed, I noticed Gry's shoes beside our bed. *Hmm, I thought, so he's making it with Gry.* I was glad and relieved, thinking it would take some pressure off me.

The next morning, Cap asked me where I'd been the night before. I told him the truth. He was really upset that I'd gone off with Süleyman. When he started screaming, I asked him what right he had to get upset since he himself had been with another woman, Gry. He was very perplexed and said he didn't understand what I was talking about. I never did find out if Cap and Gry had really been together that night. If I was wrong, what were Gry's shoes doing by the bed?

The next morning, I saw Süleyman on the beach again. We made plans to meet at Muharrem's little house at eight that evening. This turned out to be quite a joke. That evening, as usual, joints were being passed around the pension and I was stoned. I didn't have a watch, and neither did anyone else on the balcony, so I kept trying to guess the time. Then I would go down to our room and check. After that, I would sit with the others in the pension until I thought an hour had gone by, at which point I would go down to check again, only to find that ten minutes had passed. Cap wondered what I was doing. Finally, figuring it must be time to leave, I sneaked out when I got the chance. It was hilarious; trying to find Muharrem's place from the pension, I kept getting lost. Over and over I continued to make the wrong turn on a series of little paths. Of course, being stoned didn't help; I was collapsing in laughter. Eventually, I found the little hut. Süleyman wasn't there. I waited for what seemed a long time, probably only five minutes in actuality, and then decided to walk to the çay shop, Süleyman's hangout, to try to find him.

The çay shop was easier to find because it was on a main road. When I got there, Süleyman was just leaving to go meet me. It was eight o'clock. What a false conception of time I had. That night, I only stayed with Süleyman for a couple of hours. When I returned to the pension, Cap pretended that he hadn't noticed I'd been gone and was very attentive to me again. He was threatened now and playing games.

45

In the middle of the night, one of the Arabs got very sick and puked off the balcony. The group had been not only smoking but also drinking a lot. I was very sick of these people who were always throwing up, people who couldn't hold their liquor, idiots in general.

The next day, things really blew up! Cap, Clemens, and Gry decided to take a long walk down the beach, the one in frontt of the Motel Side. I told Cap I wasn't going to go along. Süleyman and I had agreed to meet on the other beach, the one on the opposite side of the village. Cap flew into a temper, yelling so loud that everyone was trying to calm him down. I told him I just didn't want to go to the beach.

"You just want to meet Süleyman, don't you?"

"No, I just don't feel like going for a walk, or being with you either."

Cap then threw such a fit that I was embarrassed to death.

I accused him of changing.

"Before, you would have been glad to go off without me for a while. You were always taking off someplace with others. What has changed?" I screamed at him. "Why do you want me to go along now?"

Of course, there was no good answer. I knew he was jealous.

Finally, to avoid any more commotion, I agreed to go along with the group. Very disgusted, I talked to Gry along the way about the problem. I told her I was envious of her and Clemens; they seemed to get along so well. She replied that everything isn't always what it seems. Hmm … totally true.

In the end, however, the walk turned out to be a lot of fun. We saw a herd of camels grazing, and we were invited into the home of some peasants. They seemed to be fascinated with us, as we were with them. I kept wondering what Süleyman would think when I didn't show up at the beach, but I figured I could find him somewhere that evening and tell him what had happened. Meanwhile, the walk took hours. When it started to get dark, Cap suggested we stop in at the Motel Side and have dinner on the way back to the village.

Berker was pleased to see us. He also seemed pleased that we'd brought friends in for some business. The motel didn't have many customers at that time; we'd been the only ones when we were there. Berker was in a gracious mood and ordered dinner for all of us, on him. What a feast. He had Turkish music playing. After eating, we had wine and fruit. Everyone was dancing. The Turkish dancing is fun, but I certainly wasn't proficient at it. It's an energetic, flamboyant dance with lots of pelvic movements.

Everyone was having a great time, and then I had a surprise. In walked Süleyman and a friend of his. I was very glad. Süleyman flashed me a look of understanding. I got the impression he had been looking for me and was glad to find me. But he sat discreetly at the other end of the long table. Cap didn't seem to guess what was going on. The dancing continued for quite a long time, and then everyone decided to take the party back to the pension (in other words, go back to smoke).

When we arrived at our pension, Ali came up to us and told the Turks, Süleyman and his friends, that they couldn't go upstairs with us. I guess the problem was that the police had been watching the pension because of the grass smoking and noise, and Ali didn't want the village people involved in it in any way. Süleyman was a bit upset by this, but he and his friends all agreed to leave. He whispered to me as he left, telling me to meet him at the coffeehouse.

Well, I tried. I tried to think of a way to leave, but nothing worked. I was wearing Süleyman's sweater that he'd lent to me when I was cold. I told Cap I wanted to go return the sweater to Süleyman. Cap knew exactly what was on my mind, of course, and refused to let me go. Instead of making a big scene, I gave up and went upstairs with the others. But I was more and more determined to get away from Cap. To think I had believed I had a "bad" relationship before. That was paradise compared to this. At least the marriage had been tolerable. Dick had been my friend. Cap was just impossible; I really couldn't stand him, and at times I was almost afraid of him. No matter what I did, he wasn't happy with me. And he continued to turn me off with his growing addiction to hashish and his behavior in general. I stayed awake late that night trying to figure out what to do.

While I was lying there thinking, Cap got up a few times to puke off the balcony. He was disgusting! He had drunk too much that night. What was new? I didn't even try to tell him to go into the toilet and not to throw up in Ali's yard wouldn't have been of any use.

Many Turks, Arabs, and Middle Easterners constantly spit, coughing up crap and spitting it out. The sound and sight were both sickening to me. Well, some of the freaks in the pension had decided to pick up that habit. Danielle was always spitting on the floor of her room; Cap had begun to spit, cough up stuff, and just become completely "natural" with all his sounds and bodily functions. Just that very day on the beach, he had urinated in full frontal view of all of us. And now he, too, was puking off the balcony into the Çobans' courtyard, when a few meters away was a toilet. To me, this was horrendous. But I was beginning to become hardened to this—just grin and bear it. What else could I do?

The next morning, I managed to get away from Cap, mainly because he was sick with dysentery. He couldn't leave the pension. I told him I'd go into the town center and see if I could find him some medicine. It was just an excuse to get away from him. Once outside, I felt free. I decided the first thing I should do would be to look for Damon, the American man, and then for Süleyman. I wanted to ask Damon if he thought it would be wise for me to leave Cap and remain by myself in Turkey.

I could find neither Süleyman nor Damon in the village center, so I waited in Mustafa's restaurant outside with a glass of *çay*. Dogan, a cute young Turk, decided to sit with me. He was full of questions about my life and about my relationship with Cap. I told him that I wasn't at all happy with Cap. Dogan suggested that I move from the pension into his. He told me I could stay free of charge and that the pension was really nice. He came on very strong. When he had finished, he had suggested quite openly that eventually our relationship would "be very strong" and that we could get married and go to the United States together. (Oh, yes?) He was quite sure that the basic feelings he had toward me were good, and indicated that we'd have a fine future together. I sat there rather in awe of the whole thing. How naïve these Turks were to think of love in these terms, how simple. I had been told previously that Dogan had been involved with a rich Frenchwoman who had paid his way to France. Obviously, it hadn't worked out, so here he was again trying his best to make it with me—and, I'm sure, countless others. I told him I knew very well what he was doing, but he just kept insisting he was serious, saying that if I changed my mind, I could always accept later.

Damon arrived on the scene about that time, so I excused myself and went to talk to him. I told him I wanted to split with Cap and asked if he felt that I'd be safe alone in Turkey. Damon had been in Side for three months. I felt he had a good feel for the place. He told me that I'd be fine in Side and recommended that I ask Muharrem for any help I might need. But he was wary of the idea of my traveling alone in the rest of the country, suggesting that I leave Side with some other tourists when I was ready. People were always coming and going; he felt I'd be able to find someone with whom to enjoy traveling for a while.

Just then, Süleyman came. I returned his sweater. He suggested we take a walk on the beach together, and I agreed. I felt quite free and determined that day; I also knew Cap was stuck in the pension. So Süleyman and I walked toward Motel Side. This turned out to be a lucky break, because two Canadian women who'd just arrived in Side, Helene and Andrea, and who were staying in Süleyman's father's pension (Pension Karga), were there that day. During the afternoon, I got to know them quite well and really liked them. I told them of my troubles with Cap and they and Süleyman suggested I move into the pension. In fact, Helene had been traveling with her boyfriend Bill, and Andrea. Bill and she had just broken up, and Bill then left alone for Istanbul. So both women were quite sure that we'd get along well, assuring me that the pension was very nice and also suggesting that we leave Side together when ready and travel farther together. Of course, Süleyman was agreeing with them on this. I liked him too, obviously, so it all seemed like a great idea.

They suggested that it would be just as well if I didn't go back to Ali's pension that night to see Cap. Süleyman said we could stay in Muharrem's little room (Muharrem could stay at his parents') and that in the morning I should go back to get my things. This seemed risky, but I agreed because I really didn't want to go back to Cap.

But the following morning, upon returning to the pension, I caught hell. About nine o'clock I went to the pension and into Cap's and my room. Cap was there and was absolutely furious. I told him as nicely as possible that I was moving to another pension, saying that he could travel by himself from now on. He tried at first to nicely convince me to stay, even saying that he was responsible for getting me back to the

States safely. (That was a joke.) He said he promised to change, and then ranted and raved. I told him I really couldn't take it anymore and started packing my things. In a fury, and in a last attempt, I guess, he threw the alarm clock against the wall, smashing it.

Meanwhile, the rest of the people in the pension had arrived at the door to see what was going on. they tried to calm Cap. I hurried with my packing, and left all the film Cap had taken, because I didn't want anything he'd done. (How I wish I'd kept it now.) And in my generosity, or in my haste to be rid of him, I even gave Cap some money, because he'd spent so much of his on hash, thinking he could smuggle it out of Turkey and earn back what he had spent, plus some. I advised him to not sell the hash, telling him to try to make it back on what he had.

And then I left.

CHAPTER 5

t last, I made it back to the çay shop and met Süleyman. He took me to my "new home," where Helene and Andrea were waiting for me. Right away, I felt a sense of family and friendship in a place that was clean and peaceful, the opposite of the place I'd just left.

Pansiyon Karga was Süleyman's father's house. The Karga family had eight children, most of whom were still living with their parents. The pension was the upstairs of the house and consisted of a large kitchen with a little two-burner gas range, a small footprint toilet, a large shower room, and two large bedrooms. One room had a fireplace. This was Helene and Andrea's room. I realized that this was the room I'd visited before, when Damon was staying there. Damon had recently moved to another pension. Between the two bedrooms, there was a medium-sized connecting room with a table. There was also an outdoor porch with a view of the sea. And it looked just as I'd remembered, spotlessly clean, whitewashed, and furnished with bright handwoven striped Turkish rugs and fabrics. I loved it!

I set myself up in my large, light, cheerful room. Soon Süleyman came upstairs with çay for all of us. Then while we sat on the balcony listening to the radio, talking, and drinking the tea, a sweet-faced woman came up the stairs. Immediately, I knew she was Süleyman's mother. Her smile was as beautiful as her son's despite the fact that she had only a few good teeth. Dressed in the typical peasant outfit of cotton printed pants covered by layers of skirts, she was always wearing a head scarf. "*Merhaba*," she said, saying hello to me with a welcoming smile. She seemed very pleased to have me there. I felt bad that I could only manage "*Merhaba*" in response.

Using sign language, she offered to wash some clothes for me. Süleyman just sat there and enjoyed the friendliness between me and his mother. Then a beautiful teenage girl with olive skin, long black hair, and gorgeous eyes arrived on the scene. She was Süleyman's sister, Fatma. After she welcomed me, she began scrubbing the floors, energetically.

My new friends and I spent the day on the beach. Süleyman made plans for Helene and Andrea to meet two of his friends whom he thought they'd like, Muharrem and Tarik.

When we got back from the beach, Süleyman went downstairs to clean up. I began to greet the rest of his family. Ali was the oldest (married and living in Side), followed by Süleyman, and then a sister I'd never met, who was also married. Fatma was the next sister. She had just gotten engaged. Then there was a brother, Cafer, about fifteen, who became my English student for a while, and then Guli (a sister about eight), followed by another brother (Kemal), maybe seven, and one more little brother, Hassan, about four.

Tarik, Fatma, Guli, and the seven-year-old brother, Kemal, became my best friends. Guli and Kemal were intent on teaching me Turkish. That first day I learned quite a few words (*sarı top*—"yellow ball," for example). I'm convinced that the best way to learn a language is to have a teacher who doesn't speak the student's language. I had no idea how to spell or read these words, so I learned just by imitating. Later, I was told that I had learned to pronounce the Turkish language quite well.

Helene, Andrea, and I quickly developed a camaraderie. Andrea, who was slightly heavy, had short curly red hair and freckles. Helene was about my height, very slender, with long straight brown hair and a quiet prettiness. Both were soft-spoken and understanding. We became better and better friends as time went on.

The first night I was there, Cap appeared on the scene. I was quite upset when I saw him coming, because I didn't know what he planned to do. He told me he'd be leaving Side in a couple of days and asked if I wanted to change my mind and go along.

"No," I said firmly. "Absolutely not!"

"I'm worried about you," he said, shaking his head. "Süleyman is married. And I just don't understand what you see in him."

Frustrated, I tried to explain what I'd already explained when I left him. "The reason I left you is not because of Süleyman, but because I can't take traveling with you anymore," I said.

But he certainly had shocked me, and now the thoughts were churning inside my head. Süleyman married? I couldn't believe this! Was Cap just lying to me to scare me? Well, he had scared me. I had absolutely no indication that Süleyman was married. He lived downstairs with his family, didn't he? Where was his wife?

Somehow, I managed to hide my surprise from Cap, who finally shrugged and left.

That night when Süleyman and I were sitting in the restaurant, I decided it was a good time to bring up the subject of his marriage. I asked him point-blank what the story was. I have to say again that the communication gap between us was quite big. Süleyman spoke some English, but in a very broken way. I had to simplify my conversation, or sometimes reword things, to get my point across. Then sometimes I'd have to guess at what he meant. In this case, he said, "Yes, I married, but it finished now." This I took to mean that he had been married but was now divorced. I told him that I had been married too—in fact, still was, as far as I knew, but it too would be "finished" very soon. Assuming now that his marriage was over, I felt a great deal of relief, because the one thing I'd always avoided like the plague was a married man. Who needs that? Besides, like I'd said before, it was obvious that Süleyman was living downstairs with his family, and I certainly hadn't seen or met a wife.

The next day, Andrea met Tarik, the same Tarik who made jewelry with Cap. Tarik's father was Turkish and his mother French; they owned the nice hotel by the sea mentioned earlier. Tarik had craggy looks, with a large bumpy nose, and was very tall with light brown hair. I felt his French genes and culture showed in his pale skin and stylish manner of dress.

The same day, Helene met Muharrem, the same Muharrem who owned the little house and greenhouse. Muharrem had rugged good looks, was quite dark and slender, and was taller than most Turks. He was very masculine, as most of the Turks seemed to be. At one time he had been a tailor, so he dressed a little more fashionably than most of the others.

It turned out that he was an interesting character. When he was a teenager, he ran away from home and went to Istanbul, looking for work. Evidently, he stayed there about a year. On his way back to Side, he was jumped by a few guys who robbed him. Muharrem was carrying a knife. In the process of defending himself, he accidentally stabbed one of the guys.. The other guys fled in fear. Muharrem was so terrified that he spent the next few months in the trees, hiding from everyone, afraid that someone would find him. How he survived, no one knew.

In general, the Turks seemed to be tough people; this is just one example. Many had knife scars from fighting. Still, Muharrem and others whom I came to know quite well, Süleyman included, were extremely gentle people and showed a great aptitude for learning—languages, facts about the world that they hadn't been taught in school. They also showed a great ability to guess what people were thinking. Basically, they seemed to possess a lot of common sense and kindness.

The first day together, the six of us took off for the beach. The weather wasn't good—too chilly and overcast for sunbathing. That day, we three Western women gained some insight into the personalities of those Turkish village men. Tarik was thirty-four, and Süleyman and Muharrem were twenty-eight. Sometimes all three acted like little kids in a very charming way, we thought. They showed off by doing acrobatics—quite well, actually. We three sat and watched and commented on how interesting and strange this was to us. An American or Canadian man just wouldn't behave like these men were—or if he did, you'd think he was really weird or egotistical. These men were just having a great time; it was obvious they were trying to impress us, but it just wasn't obnoxious. It became quite clear to me during the day that both the Canadian girls were quite attracted to these men. And I admit that I was thinking that Süleyman was pretty cute too. Mostly, though, I felt great relief because I'd gotten away from Cap.

Since the weather was so bad on the beach, we finally decided to go to Muharrem's little house for some çay. Six of us just barely fit into that place. Through the small window, we could watch the rough sea. And from a distance, I saw Cap with Clemens and Rusty. And Rusty was wearing Cap's purple pants. Someone had stolen Rusty's only pair while he was swimming, so Cap had evidently donated a pair of his. I felt very glad to be where I was and with people l really liked. I felt safe.

That day, we all smoked hash in that little house. I mentioned before that I had been smoking quite a bit in Side and that it hadn't affected me too much. But that day, I felt trapped. I have claustrophobia anyway, and that house was tiny. I told Süleyman how I felt. He quickly took me outside and walked around with me. He was very gentle and caring compared to Cap.

The next day was fantastic! First of all, Cap left town. While Süleyman and I were at the coffeehouse in the morning, Cap and the Danes came up and took the minibus out of town, headed for Istanbul. What relief I felt! Cap was wearing the necklace he'd made of beads and copper wire, a choker I think he'd intended for me, and he looked ridiculous. He felt that anything he liked, he could wear, feminine or not. And that necklace was definitely very feminine.

Süleyman had borrowed the town fisherman's boat for the day. The six of us went fishing. What an experience—it was out of another world! The boat was a large rowboat with a tiny motor. We putt-putted out to sea for a while. Then the men cast the net out over the water and began dancing in the boat. This was to attract the fish, they said. The dancing and singing was quite loud and boisterous. They jumped a lot. We three women were awed and also grateful that the boat didn't overturn. The men were singing Turkish songs and were just very uninhibited and natural, something we weren't used to. Not only did they sing, but also they made sound imitations of some of the Turkish instruments to accompany the singing. We loved it! The three men were close friends, having grown up together, and really knew how to have fun.

That day we caught one fish.

In the evening, the six of us went to the small restaurant owned by Halil, Süleyman's cousin, for a huge feast. I got to taste lots of Turkish dishes, since they were served as meze, like hors d'oeuvres—a huge spread of dishes. We ate, and danced to the Turkish music. I learned more about Turkish dancing.

That day was great. Feeling I'd gained a great deal of knowledge about Turkey, I was starting to see the country through the eyes of a Turk. When one travels with someone from one's own country, it's harder to see things in their true light. It's very valuable to meet the local people and do things with them in their way. I was really excited, since I thought that what I was doing was what travel was all about.

Now, one day just blended into another. A typical day in Side went like this: We got up about nine in the morning, sat around with a glass of çay, and then went to the beach. We'd stay at the beach until about two o'clock, and then go back into town, clean up, and change. This was also the time for writing letters, washing clothes, and doing any errands. Dinner would be about six in the evening. Then we usually would go down to the town center and sit in one of the restaurants. There was sometimes a variation of this routine, of course, but most days were something like that—very lazy, not much accomplished except for having a good time. I felt at peace finally, and decided to write a long-overdue letter to my family. I had been sending postcards with very little information, but now I felt I could tell them all that had been happening to me and what I'd been doing, also telling them that I was just fine.

March 16, 1970
Side, Turkey

Dear Family,

I'm free at last. I feel now I can write you a real, honest letter. All my letters before have been just chitchat. The truth is that Cap was making me so miserable and I hated to write home about it. But yesterday I decided to move out of the pension and go on my own. I feel like I've lost fifty pounds! That situation made my marriage look perfect. Cap showed his true colors on the trip—always completely selfish, inconsiderate, moody, with tantrums. Ugh! I thought of leaving several times and finally got up the courage to do it.

When we got to Side, we both fell in love with the place and made a lot of friends. I avoided Cap whenever possible. So I had people here to help me find a place to stay when I left Cap. I'm staying in a really nice pension (two rooms over a family house). Two Canadian girls are in the other room. I pay forty cents/night and spend a dollar a day at the most to exist. Right now, my plans are to stay in Side at least a month. From there, I don't know. I might leave with the Canadians or someone else I might meet. I feel like traveling as long as I can. It's doing wonders for me—now!

We three women are dating Turkish men—all friends. It's a fantastic, unreal experience. These men are probably the most romantic, natural, considerate, and uninhibited men any of us have ever met. They seem to fit our personalities. They're children and real men together. This village is so simple and seems not to have changed much in decades—yet they and we understand each other very well. Muharrem has a tomato greenhouse and lives in a little room large enough for a single bed and a stove and a table, period. The walls are mud. There is electricity only until 11:30 p.m. in town. They've only had it for six months! We six friends pack in the little room together, listen to records on a battery record player, and eat bread, goat cheese, and wonderful fruit. Tarik is another man. I date Süleyman, who lives downstairs in the same place I live. None of these men work steadily, only when they need money. That is typical in Turkish villages, we've heard. The three men are from highly respected families in the village. Today we took an old wooden fishing boat out to fish with nets on the sea. I felt like I'd stepped back in history! The men burst into spirited Turkish songs and dances all the time. And the boat didn't even turn over. They've even got *me singing*.

These Turkish men are so protective. I started to take a walk at nine last night, and Süleyman saw me and got quite upset. "You go to sleep now." In some ways, they're like junior high kids, but nicely so. Thank God, I got rid of Cap. My trip will be much better from now on. If I decide to leave here in a month, I'll probably leave with tourists coming through. Really nice people come here; there is no problem meeting people. I feel quite independent; it's about time. Better late than never.

The Turkish family we stay with is great. Women here always are at home and dress in many layers (pantaloons, a dress over that, and a head scarf), but they seem to like my short dresses, which I now wear only around the pension. Süleyman's mother saw my filthy "unwashable" trench coat and washed it. It's beautifully clean now. Everyone is full of smiles. They are fantastic people. So clean. I wish you could see this town and meet the people. I'm teaching Süleyman's brother English, and I'm trying to learn Turkish (slowly).

Food is wonderful here. Lots of dishes are served cold—pilaf, beans, great salads—and so cheap. On my settlement, I could live here years, even buy a house. But I won't, of course. I have many more places to go.

Süleyman says to tell you hello for him. We're sitting in a waterfront restaurant now. The wind is blowing and the water is rough. Last night I washed my hair under the cold faucet. Freezing. I'm very tan. Many days now are like our summer at home, but this is their winter.

Cap left, as I said, and so did most of the other people from the old pension. They all had so much hashish that the Turkish police were watching. I was really nervous. I have none and now feel very safe. There is a big penalty for having hashish here (thirty years!). I sometimes smoke here but never carry it around with me; it's okay. It's nothing I need certainly. No big deal. Never concern yourselves about that with me.

How are things? I think of you so much. Please write right away. It's been close to two months since I heard from you, and it's my fault since I never knew where I'd be. But I do now—so write soon. And could you please do me a favor and call a travel agent and ask what happens if I extend my excursion trip? I had round-trip on Icelandair and have to return by May 15. What happens to my ticket if I want to stay past then? I think it would be hard to find out from here.

My address here will be as follows: Büyük Postane, Side, Turkey. Please write immediately! I miss your news.

I must go. Write soon. I'll be writing more, and more regularly now.

Love,
Karen

The next day was another experience for me. Süleyman, Helene, Andrea, and I all went to the beach while Tarik and Muharrem pinched a chicken, killed it, and cooked us a meal. When we arrived at the scene, there were feathers all over. That turned me off, but I was determined to eat, even though at the time my vegetarian tendencies had begun. While we were waiting for the chicken to cook over the small burner outside, Süleyman disappeared. This was just the first of many such disappearances. Soon I began wondering what he was doing. That day, he just said he'd gone to change clothes. And when he returned, his mood seemed to have changed from carefree and happy to something much quieter. I wondered why he would change moods so quickly.

Even though they'd killed the poor chicken and that fact bothered me, the pilaf they prepared was delicious when it was finished. We sat around the pot and ate it Turkish style with hunks of bread. I had become quite used to eating out of one pot by now and enjoyed it.

We were having a great picnic together, but part of Süleyman wasn't enjoying it. Every once in a while I would glance at his somber face. I thought about what might have happened while he was gone.

But I didn't ask.

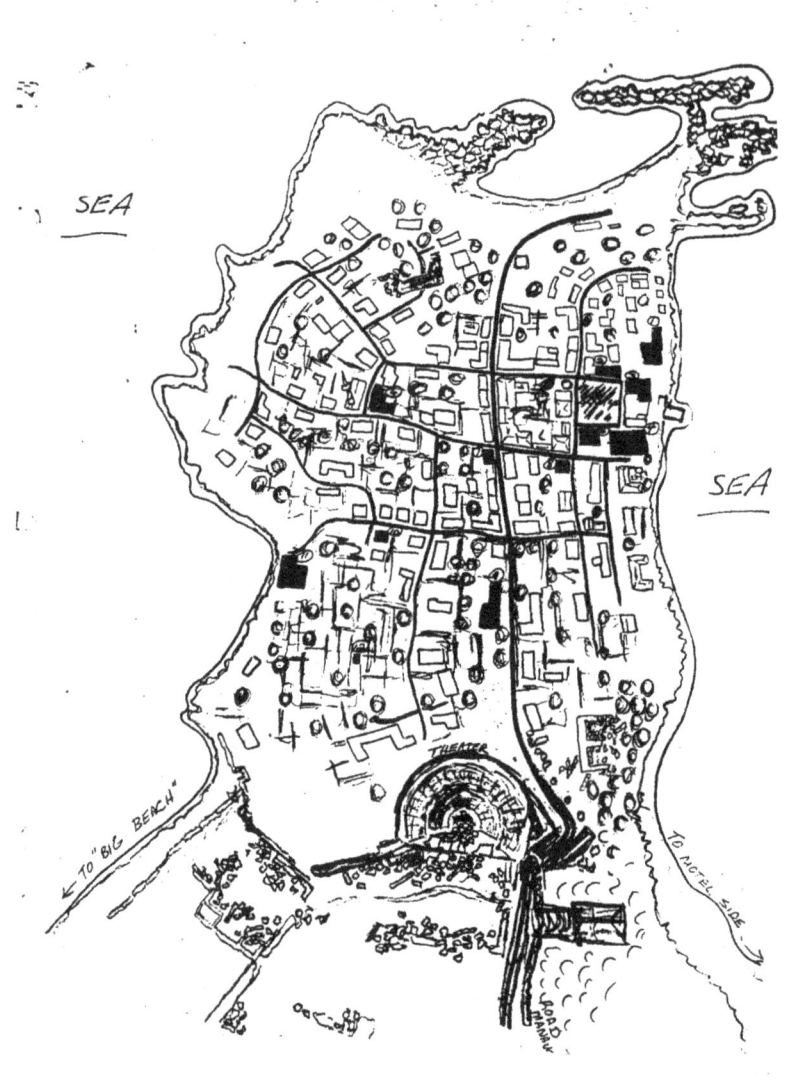

Aerial drawing of Side, Turkey

Ruins of Roman theater in Side, Turkey

View of the beach east of Side through Roman ruins

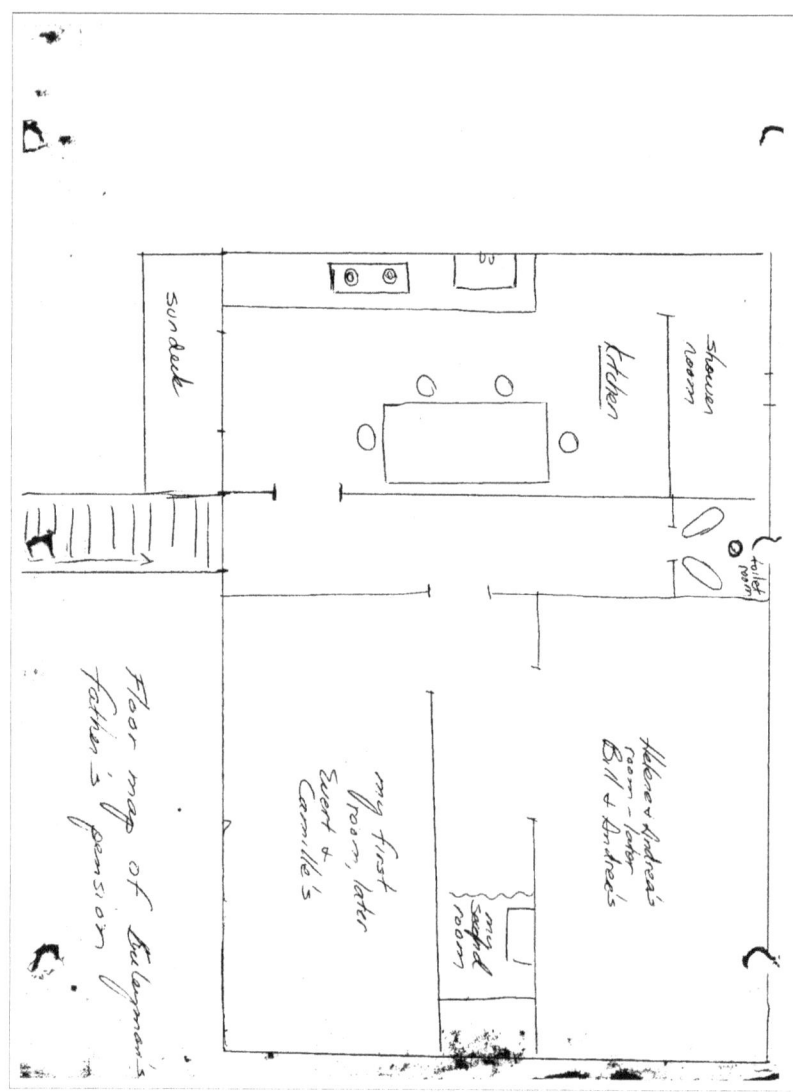

Floor plan of Pansiyon Karga

The Side coffeehouse

*Men outside coffeehouse, and the post office
in the background*

I was washing clothes the Turkish way.

Tall Evert was joking around and tried on my minidress.

KAREN CARLSON

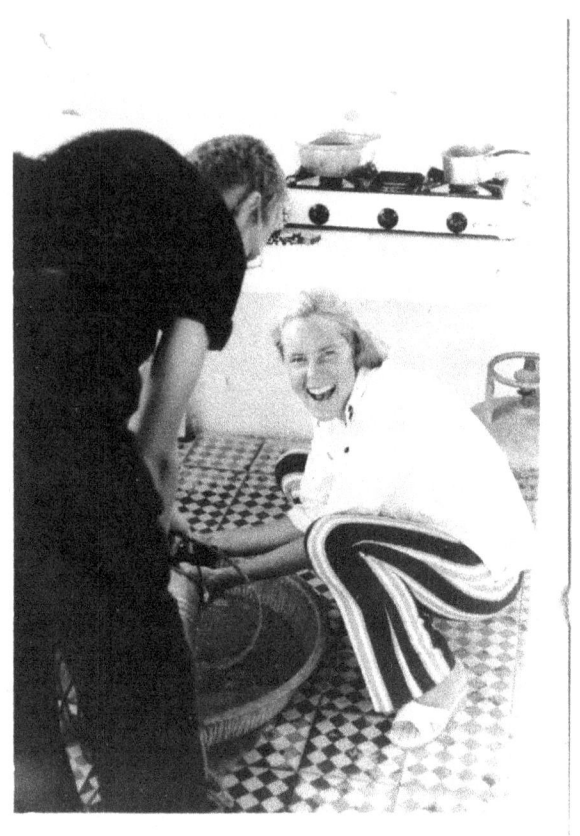

Bill adding water to my pan

65

Muharrem, Süleyman, and Andrea

A restaurant in Side

I am with Süleyman's brother and his family.

Süleyman's father, Mr. Karga

Little Turtle and I with friends

*View of village from Side
pension balcony*

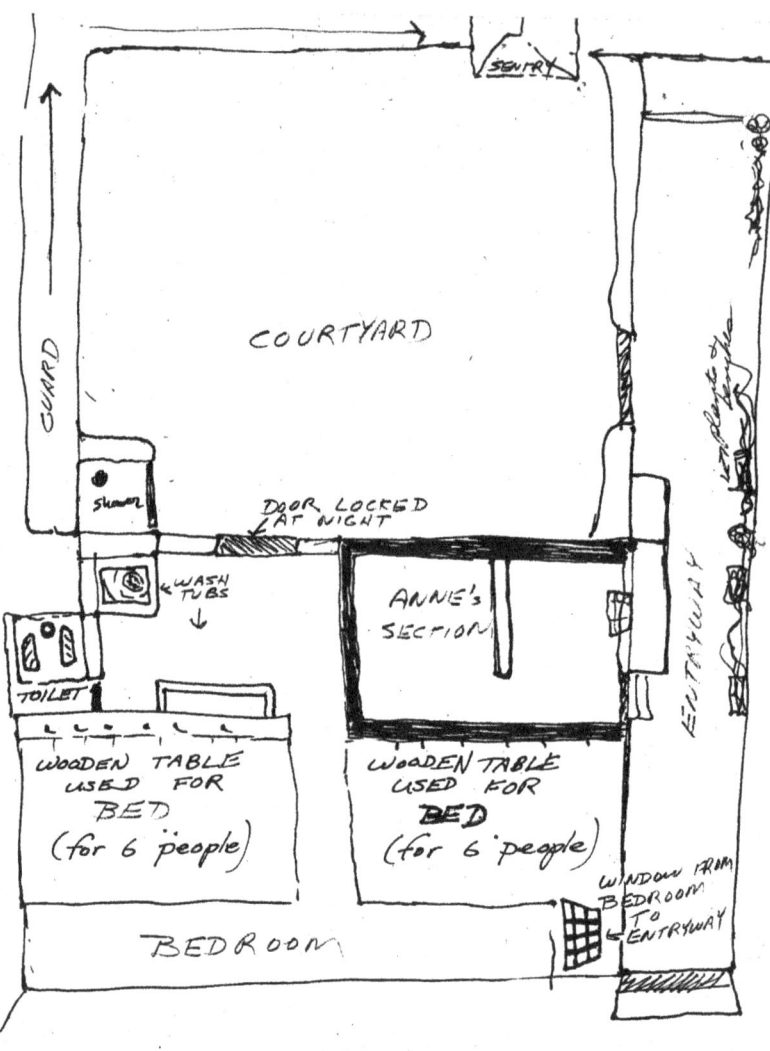

Floor plan of women's prison

Antalya, Turkey

Alanya, Turkey

CHAPTER 6

Helene and Muharrem had become very close and were spending nights together in his little house. Andrea and Tarik were not far behind in romance. Both couples would stay out late at night or spend the night together. Against my wishes, Süleyman would take me back to "my room" and tell me to go to sleep quite early at night. This was absurd; I couldn't sleep at nine. A couple of times, I asked if we could go to the discotheque or a restaurant for a while. He was quite firm about telling me I needed to sleep.

Going back to the pension alone was boring for me. But it wasn't sex I was looking for. I didn't mind at all cutting that aspect of our relationship way down. I knew he was trying to be what he thought was romantic, but instead, he was much too aggressive. So some of the sexual feelings I had for him were very quickly turned off by his roughness. Because of this, I was glad when we weren't in situations to make love. Emotionally and mentally, I was still very excited by him and by what I was learning about his culture and country. I also felt close to him because he was a very appealing person with a captivating personality. It was a challenge and yet a lot of fun explaining to him all the many things about my world that he didn't know. But while I leaned on him a lot for companionship of various sorts, I didn't really mind having to spend my nights alone. But why couldn't we spend time with the others dancing or just sitting around in the restaurants drinking tea? I didn't understand.

At any rate, because of his frequent disappearances for short periods of time, I found myself getting quite curious, and also quite uncomfortable. Things weren't like they should be; there were strange vibes. And as time went on, I learned more about Süleyman and what he was doing when he disappeared for periods of time. When Helene talked to me one day, she said Muharrem had told her that what Cap had told me was true. Süleyman was still married. However, he and his wife were separated. Harika, his wife, lived in a house attached to the pension. In the beginning of the marriage, Süleyman used to stay there with her, but very soon returned to his parents' house to live. The marriage had been arranged; there had been twin babies and they had died. There was speculation about why they had died, but no one seemed to know why. Süleyman had been involved with countless tourists, like me, and had repeatedly ordered his wife to leave and go back with her parents in the village. Several times she had done so but had always returned. Muharrem said that Süleyman felt quite strongly about me, unlike the others he'd been with (those had been purely sexual, he said). He said that now there was lots of discussion going on in the family about the marriage and how to end it. The wife, Harika, was considered strange, I guess; Süleyman's family didn't like her.

But the thing that got me when I heard this was that now Harika had returned to the little house and was living just meters away from me, she had obviously seen Süleyman and me together. It was too much; I just couldn't believe it.

The first chance I had to talk to Süleyman, I did.

"Süleyman, you are still married and your wife is living in that little house at the pension. People have told me this. You told me your marriage was finished."

"Yes. That all correct," he replied. "My wife live that house. I not sleep with her. I sleep in big house."

Still upset, I told him I definitely didn't want to be involved in this sort of situation. He said it was no problem at all. Divorce was difficult in Turkey, but he was working on it. The trouble had started long before me; it had been an arranged marriage and he had never loved it.

I was still extremely worried, but figured that if his seeing me didn't upset his family and that his friends accepted it, maybe it was all right. We weren't doing anything more than friendship-type things in public. We'd been seen together all over the village—and I hadn't been the first woman. I decided that public opinion was the important thing. And since Harika and he were separated, it was all right. After all, I was still legally married too.

Then Süleyman told me, "I like you too much." This, I discovered, was his way of saying he loved me. Like and love in Turkish are expressed by the same word. *Too* is often used instead of *very* by people learning English. Still, whatever, I didn't want Süleyman to feel much for me since I considered this whole thing an experience and just a way of having fun while I was in Turkey. I didn't know how to explain that to him, but I figured it wasn't important. I wasn't going to stay in Side forever.

After all this discussion with Helene and Süleyman, I still didn't have the answer to my question. If, in fact, it was true that Süleyman was finished with his wife, why did he keep leaving me here and there for short periods of time? He always had some excuse—he was going to change clothes or tell his mother something—but it didn't make sense to me.

One afternoon I was on the balcony. Fatma and Guli were in the yard with an older girl. Since I'd never seen her before, suddenly I had the suspicion that she might be Harika. Fatma and Guli smiled at me and said a few words in Turkish, and then pointed at the older girl. Deciding to ask who it was, I said, *"Kızkardeş?"* (Sister?), pointing at the older girl. At first, they shook their heads no, but then once I repeated the question, they said yes. They weren't sure how to explain how she was related to them. I knew very little Turkish, but I just knew it was Harika. I was shocked—Harika was plain, tall, clumsy-looking, and clad in the village costume. I couldn't imagine this was Süleyman's wife. Harika just sat there, staring off into the distance and not paying any attention at all to us on the balcony.

One night Süleyman came upstairs with me to my room. He had been there just a short time when we heard someone coming up the stairs. I saw it was Süleyman's father. He bent over Süleyman and whispered something, and then walked out. Süleyman explained to me that he had to leave and in fact didn't explain why. He quickly left. I lay there wondering what was happening. Soon after, I heard steps again and the door opened. I felt like screaming. What was the father doing? He walked over to me. I was terrified. Then he whispered something softly: "Süleyman *burada çok fena.*" Then quickly he walked out, leaving me mystified. What was happening? Was Süleyman all right? I knew "Süleyman *burada çok*" meant "Süleyman here very," but I didn't know the word *fena*. I stewed over this all night. Andrea had a Turkish dictionary, but since the electricity was out and I didn't know where the lantern was, it was useless. Besides, she might have been sleeping. So I waited.

The next morning I checked the dictionary. *Fena* meant "bad." So the father had told me, "Süleyman here very bad." Thinking I knew what that meant, I confronted Süleyman about it that day. He assured me that his father was worried about his coming up to my room and how it would look; he decided that he shouldn't do it anymore. I put it all down to Turkish morals and didn't worry about it.

Sunday, March 22, 1970
Side, Turkey

Dear Family,

You can't imagine how anxiously I'm waiting to hear from you. I think my letter with my address ought to be in the United States by now. So maybe I'll have to wait another week. I really can't wait. I've had many fears that something might be wrong there. I want to know you're all right.

This last week really has been beautiful; I can't get over this place. I feel like I'm in another world—so far removed from things I used to care about (material things, comforts, like hot water, cars, and news). Every once in a while, I hear some news on *Voice of America. Other than that, it's all so far away. I haven't seen another American (except Cap before he left) for weeks.*

I'm sitting on my balcony in the sun with Süleyman's portable radio. I can see the sea from here, a few yards away, and the blue snow-covered mountains in the background. Turkey is very rocky. Süleyman's mother is hanging out wash (including my things) on the rock fence and trees in the yard. I can see Roman ruins on the other side. This place is such a gorgeous paradise. Süleyman brought me a plate of hot macaroni and goat cheese a while ago. I also had sunflower seeds and some raw green nuts.

Getting rid of Cap really has freed me. I kept wondering why I was so depressed and miserable so often. It just doesn't work traveling with a male "friend" when you don't even have the same values or interests. Anyway, I realize now that I need to be free. I want to live and experience, and to experience all I want, I must be free. I have no fear of being alone now. If I feel like marrying again sometime, I know I'll be able to find a person I want and who wants me. Most people my age are married and have children, but I really don't care.

I plan now to stay in Side at least until August. I really have to, financially speaking. I have $220 left. I might go to Istanbul or somewhere else for a short time, and then come back to Side. This town is really supposed to swing in the summer. They're building new restaurants now. I hate to see this village become commercial, which it's bound to do in a few years.

The situation with Süleyman here is really strange. His and his wife's family arranged the marriage five years ago. They have lived in a little house that is attached to his family's, but have separated twice. Even though Süleyman has repeatedly asked his wife to leave, she returns. She is village-like in customs and dress. Neither he nor his family can stand her, I guess. Divorce is difficult in Turkey—and expensive. Anyway, she is here now, so he sleeps at his parents' and is never home. I didn't realize all this when I first went out with him. I thought he was divorced. Communication between us isn't perfect since his English isn't great. He said the marriage was "no problem" and "finished," and since he openly dated me, I thought he meant he was divorced. Anyway, his family has really taken to me and knows that we see each other. They do my wash, give me food, and are really beautiful to me.

Today I've seen and heard much arguing downstairs. I think they are trying to make the wife leave. God! It's taken me a week to try to sort this out. The thing is that Süleyman is quite modern and his wife is Old World. I just can't believe his family is so liberal in thought to understand his wanting to be free and date me. I know he has had lots of tourist girlfriends. I also know that he's becoming hung up on me. Somehow I always get involved with men who like me more than I really want them to. But Süleyman is, I think, the most romantic and thoughtful, yet completely male, man I've encountered. If I sense this marriage thing is becoming too much, I'll go somewhere else where living is cheap. I always said I'd never date a married man, and I meant it. But there are so many things I didn't understand here. At least I know town and family are on my side. There's no doubt about that. The two Canadian girls and their two men are going strong (those men are single), and the girls plan to stay indefinitely too. Turkey is a good base for travel since it's close to Europe, Africa, and on into Asia. I think I told you I could work nights at the discotheque starting in a month with Süleyman, for low pay of course. Really I am living day by day now and am watching this marriage thing with an eagle eye.

Monday, March 23

I find my English deteriorating a little from talking to Turks and other people who don't speak perfect English. "I go" instead of "I am going," etc. The Canadians are doing it too.

I'm getting Turkish in my dress when it's chilly—pants under dresses. Turkish men are possessive and jealous and very passionate in their moods. Süleyman hates a short sweater of mine that shows my middle when I bend over. But he likes bikinis on the beach. He said last night, "If anyone speaks bad to you, I will take my pistol and kill." This was said very seriously, and I swear I believe him. However, he doesn't have a pistol (as far as I know). I see that the Turkish men have pent-up violence, and I wonder if it's partially due to the huge difference between the men's and women's roles. Yesterday he kissed me in front of his mother while she stood there beaming. It really shook me up. Now she's fighting with his wife again. Wow! I wish I understood the language. I don't want to get too involved in this. I think Süleyman is fantastic, but I have no intention of a future with him. Our worlds are miles apart. He's never been out of Turkey except for Cyprus. He has no conception of what I really am. I think I am adapting well to the customs and food here—but temporarily. It's just part of my travel experience. I'll try to explain that to him, but how? Maybe the best thing is not to commit myself in any way when he talks about my staying indefinitely.

I know I'm talking on and on about my thoughts, which I'm doing because I want you to know everything. You're all my family and deserve to know what I'm doing. I know my life is pretty strange sometimes and I want you to know about it. You have an invitation to Turkey for the summer from Süleyman. I'd love for you to come here, but I realize it's probably impossible. How are your London plans coming along? I hope I hear from you soon. I miss all of you very much.

Love,
Karen

Süleyman was fun to be with in lots of ways. I especially got a kick out of the language barrier between us, working on both his English and my Turkish. One morning when he came to the pension to wake me, he said, "*Hadi, kalk.*" I said, "What?" I thought he was speaking English and had said, "Hottie cock." Finally, I understood he'd said in Turkish, "Let's go. Get up."

Here's another quotation from him, "For six months electric city come Side," meaning that Side had had electricity for six months.

And another: "After one hour you left from me, my heart was not in same place; it was working out of my body."

Speaking with him was often very amusing because of the language barrier. Both of us could laugh easily at each other.

One day Süleyman and I went to the beach and met another couple, an American woman, Camille, and a Dutch man, Evert. They had been traveling together since they'd met in Istanbul and had come to Side. They weren't involved romantically, though, they said. Since they hadn't yet found a place to stay, Süleyman encouraged them to come to the pension. There was room for both of them in my room, but Süleyman insisted on fixing up the middle area between the two bedrooms for me instead. He just didn't want me sleeping in the same room with another man, whether or not I was involved with him. I decided it didn't matter. I'd have more privacy in my little nook anyway. Besides, I wasn't sure at the time that Evert and Camille weren't really involved, as they said.

So Evert and Camille arrived and took over my room. Süleyman blocked off the window end of the middle area with a drawstring curtain, and the couch there became a bed for me.

I really liked Evert and Camille. Evert was tall and slender, had gorgeous blue eyes, and was really cute. He had a long dramatic mustache and wore very fashionable clothes. I particularly liked his gorgeous brown leather jacket. Evert spoke in a singsong Dutch accent and said he was frustrated because no one spoke Dutch but the Dutch; it taxed his brain to have to speak English all the time.

Camille was large, husky, and very much an extrovert.

Evert had just come from Istanbul and said he'd met Cap at the Blue Mosque. Cap had recommended he come to Side, telling him about all the young travelers who went there. According to Evert, Cap had been lying on the grass with other freaks and the police had asked them to leave. Cap told the policeman off and Evert felt embarrassed. It was typical of Cap to act like that. Again, I was very happy I'd ended our relationship.

April 3, 1970
Side, Turkey

Dear Family,

Thank God, I got your letter. I've never in my life been so excited to get a piece of mail. I'd had a nightmare the night before that something bad had happened to you. Süleyman said that meant I'd get a letter the next day, and he was right. So good! The address, just Side, Turkey, made it, but I guess the longer one is better.

Last week an American woman and a Dutch man moved into the pension. We're all really having a great time. Evert, the Dutch man, and a Canadian man are probably going to the Middle East in a week. I could go along, but I think I won't. Your letter scared me. It's funny. We're here right on top of the war and don't know what's happening. Süleyman did hear on the radio that there was bad fighting yesterday. I really want to go to those countries, but I guess maybe I shouldn't.

I'm miserable because my movie camera is broken and no one in Turkey (or at least close to Side) can fix it. I took it to Antalya and they broke it further. Evert knows cameras and said it's a minor repair (five to six dollars), but he doesn't have the equipment to fix it himself here. He's a photographer. This country and things that are happening would make the most phenomenal movies. I'm sick that I can't fix it. Evert said I'd have to go to a European city.

Now I'm trying to decide what to do. I still can come back on my ticket by May 15. If I don't, I'm really stuck here until August (financially). I can't go to the places I want (Middle East). On the other hand, it's a nice, easy, lazy life here. I now know more about Turkey than any place except the United States. I'm constantly with Turks or Europeans. I'm learning so much about people, life, and human relations. I'm afraid I might regret it if I go back in May, even though at times here I am bored and I miss you and comforts and variety of US life. And, again, I hate not being able to take movies so I'll be able to remember the many details.

The situation here is still interesting. I now have Süleyman's marriage story and everything now makes sense. Everything is in the open, and the wife is still around although Süleyman never goes to his house. He's now trying to round up money for a divorce. At any rate, as Aunt Loretta told you, "Turks are charming." He's got a good mind, I can tell, but his world and mine are impossibly far apart. He likes me a lot, seriously, but I'm explaining to him as best as possible how impossible a future with me would be. This is just an experience for me, but I can't say that, of course. Naturally, I like him a lot too—for a while.

A butcher lives next door. Last week we stood on our balcony and watched him slaughter a cow and clean it. What a gross, unreal sight. I can't believe I was able to stand there and watch that happening. Then the next evening, Süleyman and I went to dinner at a Turkish friend's, and guess what we ate? That cow. Really, a year ago I wouldn't have touched it. This trip has conquered some of my previous hang-ups. I've even helped sick drunks walk home. I still hate it, but I can put up with it now.

The weather today is awful. Days like today I get bored. I think Easter was last Sunday. Anyway, lots of tour buses came through that day, and Süleyman and I sat on the Roman theater and watched them climb all over the ruins. Sometimes I really feel like I belong here instead of being a tourist myself. It's funny. I think tourists will spoil this village in a few years. The first tourists came here five years ago.

The minaret is across the street, and the muezzin who does the call to prayer is a riot. He stops and coughs every so often. It's really funny.

We've decided restaurant eating is too "expensive" (maybe thirty-five to fifty cents for dinner—a big dinner). So Süleyman cooks for the two of us. It's amazing what he can do with almost nothing. I can cook too, but I need recipes and modern conveniences. But we eat a lot of starches and bread. I feel like I'm gaining weight. That's not good.

Excuse the word *fuck to follow; I guess you realize it's become very common. Plus, it's one of the first things Turks learn to say in English. Süleyman and I were out in a field sitting looking at the sea. We heard a faint repeated sound. He said, "Listen! Turtles are fucking." I laughed and said, "Sure." He walked a couple of yards and said, "Come here." I went and in a ditch, where there were two turtles "fucking." I couldn't believe that small sound would tell him that. It was really funny. He then went into a detailed description of many kinds of animals fucking (from camels to donkeys), and it really pointed out to me what a citified naïve person I am. It was interesting and hilarious.*

Thanks a lot for your çok güzel (very good) letter. I know a lot of single Turkish words, but I can't make sentences. It's a difficult language. I'm waiting anxiously for your next letter.

Love,
Karen

I was so impressed with the turtle incident that I gave Süleyman the nickname Little Turtle. When I called him that, he appeared to enjoy it. Also, it was easier for me to say "Little Turtle" than "Süleyman" (which to me was difficult to pronouunce correctly).

One evening, Süleyman and I went with Evert and Camille to Mamadou's restaurant. Mamadou was Süleyman's cousin, one of his many relatives in Side. The evening started out fine. The Turks were drinking raki, similar to Greek ouzo. Made from grapes and aniseed, raki is a very popular, very strong Turkish drink. The Europeans and I couldn't drink the raki, so we settled on wine. I'd never before been with Süleyman when he was drinking. I found he and Cap had something in common after all. He got obnoxiously drunk and talked more and more loudly. Finally, he got violent and started smashing records on the floor. This was done for no reason at all that I could see. Early in the evening, Evert said he was tired and went back to the pension. I wished Camille and I had followed him then.

Everyone in the restaurant—Arif, the waiter; Süleyman's cousin; and several other tourists—were very embarrassed by Süleyman's behavior. At last he disappeared outside and didn't return for a while. Arif said he was being sick. When he returned, he continued drinking, and then disappeared outside again. Camille and I decided to leave. She insisted that we get Süleyman home, so we walked through the village with Süleyman between us, hobbling along. At one point, he stopped, opened his pants, and took a piss right there. I was truly thankful that he didn't vomit there too. I was very disgusted with him, even though he continued to insist he was fine.

When we arrived at the pension, a surprise was waiting for us. Harika was there. She didn't say a word, just disappeared with Süleyman into the parents' house. Evert was still up. The three of us sat outside on the balcony for hours that night, talking. Occasionally we could hear the horrible sound of Süleyman's being sick downstairs.

Both Evert and Camille also tried to understand exactly what was happening with Süleyman and his wife. They, too, were worried about it, but felt that what I was doing was all right. Still, it was a puzzle to us all. What was going on? The language barrier was so great.

The next morning, Süleyman came upstairs to wake me; I told him to get out. He just smelled like wine and he turned me off completely. To me, he was starting to behave just like Cap. I was completely repelled. I went to the beach with Evert and Camille, and in the early afternoon Süleyman appeared, all smiles. He felt that the night before was a joke.

Camille, Evert, and I tried to straighten him out, explaining to him that behaving that way was childish and obnoxious.

All of us explained to Süleyman our feelings about drinking. Sometimes he seemed to be the strongest one of us all and in control, and at other times, like this time, we seemed to be leading him. He promised to watch his drinking from then on. I told him I'd leave Side if he began drinking heavily again. And I meant it.

By this time, Helene was virtually living at Muharrem's. It was a good thing, because her old boyfriend, Bill, the one she'd traveled with to Side, had returned. He came back partly to see if he could win her back and partly because he loved Side too. He moved into Andrea's room and then had to be told gently that Helene was with Muharrem. He seemed to accept this calmly and with resignation. And then the three of them became friends.

Bill was such a creep. His presence added some more character to the pension. He was tall and slender, and had curly blond hair that had been recently cut so as not to irritate the conservative Turkish border officials. He wore glasses and looked the bookworm type. And his clothing was terrible; he always wore baggy black pants and a black shirt. While in Side, he bought some striped material and had the tailor make him some pants. Then all the Turks laughed at him, since Turks use the material he'd chosen for men's pajamas. In the warm, sunny weather, he looked hot and uncomfortable and ugly. Also, he was the grossest eater. None of us could stand eating around him. Every bite he took was very noisy. And his burps!

Bill had the habit of hanging around when a meal was being prepared. Usually some of us would go out and buy the ingredients. Süleyman would contribute from the kitchen downstairs, and then he would cook for us. Bill never contributed anything, but he'd always be there when we sat down to eat, making us feel guilty if we didn't invite him, which we usually ended up doing. Soon, this irritated all of us; he just didn't share anything.

He also had the habit of drinking raw eggs every morning. Poor Bill! I'm really criticizing him, but he certainly was the subject of much conversation and aggravation around the pension. Other than all these bad qualities, he was a pretty nice, fairly intelligent man. Still, I always wondered what Helene had seen in him.

Since I'd run out of my American shampoo, I bought a Turkish shampoo to try. This was a disaster. My hair turned into greasy strings. At first, I thought it was just wet, and then I realized that it was never going to dry. Camille came to my rescue and let me use some French shampoo that she had brought along with her. What a difference it made. I hadn't known that really bad shampoos existed. I was continually learning.

Time continued to pass, and Süleyman continued with his little disappearing acts. I had begun to realize that he was trying to put up an "innocent" front, not always being with me, coming into town from the beach by a different route, and so on. This was smart, I realized, but I got sick of being left by the theater, for instance, for an hour while he went to discuss ideas about the divorce, or whatever he was doing, with his father. I didn't feel like I had to be with him all the time, but I disliked going somewhere with him and then having him disappear with the promise, "I be back just ten minutes." And then he wouldn't return for a half hour or so. What I didn't realize then was that he and his father were working on a plan to get rid of Harika.

All of us in the pension would sit for hours on the balcony and talk. Often Harika would be in the yard below. Several times we saw her just sitting there playing with rocks in the dirt. Always, she would smile up at us. We couldn't figure it out. Was she retarded? Why did she smile at me? How naïve was she?

Meanwhile, Evert and I became quite close. He was very much fun to be with. I enjoyed his company. A photographer, he was traveling then to get pictures of the Middle East. He had plans to go on to Israel and Egypt, and across North Africa, after leaving Turkey. Bill wanted to go to these places too, and so did I. We talked of going together. Evert said I could go along, but he added the caveat that he wouldn't want to have to be responsible for me. He felt he would have enough problems taking care of himself in those countries, especially because he was a photographer. I told him I'd think about it, since I was very tempted to go.

One day, Bill left for Istanbul and said he'd return in a couple of days. He wanted to order some sheepskin coats for his family and figured he'd get a better buy in Istanbul. Evert was going to wait in Side for Bill to return, and then they planned to leave for the Middle East together. Camille was in love with a US Army officer stationed in Germany and was going to go back to Europe to be with him. (So it was true that she and Evert had a platonic relationship.) Camille was going to travel to Athens, and then go quickly to Germany; she kept encouraging me to leave with her.

Actually, I was ready to leave Side too; I was anxious to travel some more, and while the relationship with Süleyman was nice at times and extremely interesting, I knew there was no future and so I didn't see a lot of reason to stay.

But Evert's offer turned me off. I knew he was intending to take risks and that he was worried about my maybe going along, although he encouraged me to at times. But in the next moment, he'd mention problems my presence might cause. I certainly didn't want to go with Camille, because she was just going to cover ground I'd already seen. Finally, I decided to wait it out. Helene and Andrea still thought they might leave in a month or so, and I figured I'd go with them then. And, though I didn't like to admit it to myself, I knew I would hate leaving Süleyman.

CHAPTER 7

*S*ome Belgians—Chantal, Etienne, their children—and another female friend arrived in Side. Their arrival was an event since, according to gossip, Chantal had slept with Süleyman the summer before. Everyone was talking about this and was interested to see what would happen this time.

Chantal was a sexy blonde with roving eyes. Her husband, Etienne, was a rich factory owner. A few years prior, he had been badly burned in his factory and had terrible scars on his face. I found it hard to look at him.

Süleyman told me about Chantal. As was the case with him and "many other girls," they had made love. Süleyman said it had been "only to jump" (have sex, his Turkish-English). Süleyman was constantly trying to make me believe he'd never loved another woman and that all his other relationships had been only about sex. This didn't impress me because I didn't care that much. So what? I didn't want him to feel strongly about me anyway. Also, it didn't impress me that he may have been having sex with anyone and everyone without feelings or caring. But Muharrem and Tarik, who kept telling me that my affair with him was different for Süleyman, backed up his statements of real love for me.

At any rate, Chantal was always around—on the beach, at the discotheque, at the restaurant. She had a "come on" look like I'd never seen before. But this year, she chose another Turk for her fun. Everyone felt sorry for Etienne. But maybe he was making it with Chantal's friend. Who knows?

During this time, Evert and I became closer and closer. He was worried about Süleyman's and my relationship. "What is going on downstairs?" he'd ask. He had the feeling that something was very wrong, but when we discussed Süleyman, he just couldn't say why he felt that way. I had the same feeling. But neither of us thought that I should stop seeing Süleyman. It was a sticky, weird thing, and we both knew the language barrier caused a lot of the problem. Evert felt I'd be all right in Side, though, and that sort of confirmed my thoughts. Plus, in the United States or Holland, there wouldn't have been much of problem, I'm sure. But this was Turkey—and quite different. I just didn't realize how different.

I ended up spending a lot of time with Evert. Camille left for Istanbul and then Athens. Bill was gone; Andrea and Tarik were never around the pension. Süleyman was there and then not there. I spent lots of time with him, but there was a lot of time when he was downstairs. To make things look very innocent, after things closed down in the village at nine at night, he would take me home and then go home himself. Since I'm a night owl and so was Evert, we'd sit up talking over glasses of çay or reading for hours by the light of the gas lanterns.

Then Süleyman began to get jealous of Evert. I told him that was ridiculous, that Evert and I were just friends. Actually, Evert had talked of getting involved with me but said that he was afraid of Süleyman and his reaction. I understood because I felt the same way; there wasn't any point to it, especially not for the short time that we'd have together anyway. Besides, I did care about Süleyman enough to keep me from getting very interested in Evert romantically. So the situation was genuinely platonic. I tried to convince Süleyman of that.

One day on the beach, Süleyman and I were discussing Evert. He told me that he'd seen Evert sitting on my bed while I was in bed and that Evert had tried to kiss me. This was true. While Camille and Bill were still in Side, everyone drank quite a bit of wine one night. After I went to bed, Evert came over, sat on my bed, and talked to me. He did try to kiss me. I shoved him aside. It's a good thing I did, because it turned out that Süleyman had been spying on me for a number of nights. He'd gotten a ladder and climbed up to peek through the window. Since my bed was in front of the window, he had a good view. I was furious; this was ridiculous. First of all, I was innocent, and second of all, the very idea that he was spying on me every night was absurd. I was indignant. But Süleyman insisted that when I had refused Evert's kiss, he decided to trust me. This incident made me all the more aware of the huge gap between us: communication, ideas about relationships between men and women, and friendships.

I did finally convince Süleyman, however, that Evert and I were just friends, so I continued spending a lot of time with Evert. There were a few rainy days when we just sat and played cards all day and drank çay. Sometimes, we'd get hungry and go splurge on a bowl of çorba (soup)—fifteen cents.

I realize, writing this years later, that I may be stressing the bad things about my relationship with Süleyman. Obviously, there was a lot of good or else I wouldn't have kept on with it. Probably the best thing to me was what I was learning about a way of life and thinking than completely different from any I'd ever known. Also, Süleyman was a very charming man. Everybody liked him. It's true that he did have his faults, including a drinking problem and temper. But it was a rare day when he would drink. And compared to what I'd been through with Cap, Süleyman seemed nearly perfect to me. Usually, he was the life of the place and a lovable person. And he was a smiling, adorable guy. Yes, I was in love with my Little Turtle, most of the time.

One day, Tarik had a big argument with Muharrem that we tourists didn't understand. Süleyman sided with Muharrem, which put Andrea, Helene, and me in a spot. Tarik didn't want Andrea to associate with us because he was furious with Süleyman and Muharrem. It was a childish thing, we thought; none of us could really understand what was going on. A couple of times, Tarik came to the pension to pick up Andrea, and Süleyman ordered him off the property. Finally, Tarik found another pension for Andrea. Of course, Andrea saw Helene and me anyway. The quarrel had seemed pointless, but it was never resolved as far as I know. Those three guys had been friends all their lives until that disagreement.

One rainy and miserable day, Evert was very antsy because Bill was late in returning to Side. Süleyman appeared early in the morning that day to have *çay* with us, and then I didn't see him again until before dinner. Evert and I sat inside playing cards and more cards. When

Süleyman returned, I asked him what was going on. He acted very mysterious. He said, "I can't see you today. I fixing everything. Don't worry." Evert and I were mystified. About nine o'clock, Evert and I decided to walk down to the restaurant for some *çorba*. When we got back, Süleyman ran up, said a few unintelligible things, and hurried away. This was followed by the sound of an argument downstairs. Evert and I looked out the window and could see Süleyman pacing up and down the street in front of the house. I had an eerie sense of mystery and apprehension. What was going on?

The next day, I found out. Süleyman appeared upstairs and ecstatically announced that he'd locked his wife out of his house. He had returned her dowry to her and taken her key. The house his, he had been determined to get her out. His parents had been behind this. Everyone seemed to be celebrating. Evert and I felt some relief; it seemed that this had been the right, and a very positive, thing to do (in that country anyway). Süleyman and his father went to Manavgat that day and signed the house over to his father; this would presumably guarantee that Harika couldn't trespass since the house was no longer her husband's. Everyone in the family was very happy.

One day, Süleyman and I got a temporary job offer. A tour group was due to visit Side and had made reservations at Mamadou's restaurant for lunch. Muharrem, Süleyman's cousin, asked Süleyman to help out that day as a waiter. Süleyman agreed, so I went along. Tables were set up outside, as usual, but white tablecloths were on the tables and each table had a vase of fresh flowers in the center. I stood at the outside bar and changed records for Mamadou. The tour group appeared. There were many Americans among them. A couple of young women came up to me and asked what I was doing there. I explained that I was a traveler. They wondered how long I was going to stay in Side; I said I didn't know, maybe through the summer. They were shocked and impressed, and wondered if I were homesick. I had the strangest feeling when I talked with them. They seemed like they were from a different world entirely. For a long time now I had been with people who just took traveling and being away from home for granted. Those young women made me feel like a Turk; we really were on different wavelengths.

For our reward for the work we had done, Süleyman and I got to go into the kitchen and eat as much as we wanted. What a treat. The food was delicious, and it seemed like such a luxury to have such giant servings of everything. When we returned to the pension, Evert was quite envious of what we'd done.

Tuesday, April 7, 1970
Side, Turkey

Dear Family,

Here I am again. Got your second letter this morning after hearing last night I had a letter. But the post office was closed. Such anticipation.

Thanks so much for sending the camera. I'll have a roll of film developed here to make sure they haven't x-rayed it. I'm hoping I won't have to pay a lot of duty. I get different opinions from people here.

I'm sitting here laughing to myself again. The muezzin is coughing. Maybe the mosque people think he has a good voice so they let him sing despite his cough. Or maybe he's high-ranking or something. I don't know anything about the Muslim religion.

I'm glad spring is coming there. I've been in perpetual spring–early summer since early February now. The Turks still consider this winter. It's probably 75°–80°F today, and it's often hotter.

You asked about things to buy in Side. There are two tiny shops here that sell hand-embroidered clothes, woven bags for purses, and some alabaster and brass things. In Antalya, a larger town close by, you can buy long woven runner rugs for five dollars. I haven't really looked around a lot since I've mostly been in Side. In Istanbul, the big thing is suede coats (twenty to thirty dollars) and gorgeous goat and sheepskin coats (same price). I think I'll bring a white one back (long fur inside, skin on outside). Everything is inexpensive here. What kind of things would you like? Oh yes, there is lots of copper-turquoise bead jewelry, handmade and simple.

Don't worry. I've scored a victory with the possessiveness and jealousy problem between Süleyman and me. After several hours talking on various occasions, I finally won. I think the problem was that the Turks aren't used to "free" women. I told him that I would do nothing with anyone else unless I had already broken up with him because we didn't get along anymore. I would do nothing behind his back. I explained that Europeans and Americans could have friendships with the opposite sex. All this produced miraculous results. He understood. I can now be friendly with others and there is no anger.

May 21, my three-month visa for Turkey runs out, so I'll have to either leave the country and come back or buy a residence permit if I want to stay. I'm tentatively thinking of going to Athens again in hopes that someone there can fix my movie camera. I really don't want to leave Turkey, and especially Side, until I have movies of it. It's such an exotic place.

I'm also trying to decide just what to do with myself. I run through all moods, ecstatically happy to depressed. Then I feel dependent, then independent. When I miss the security of my marriage, I quickly remember the frustration I felt. At least I never feel that now. When I'm feeling independent, I think of staying over here for maybe a year—after the summer going to London or Amsterdam and working. Evert, my Dutch friend, thinks I could easily work in Holland with Manpower or another such agency because of my office skills. With the money I'll get in August and working some, I could live quite a while and travel some too. Now I'm spending time here, but only seeing one place. I really want to see more. So I don't know. My only motivation to go home right now is to see you.

Süleyman begins working tomorrow at one of the village restaurants, which means we will both eat free now. That means forty-five cents/night expense to live, except for stamps or miscellaneous things I buy. Süleyman is a great cook and makes delicious things out of almost nothing, but I eat too much, especially since most of it has a pasta or potato base. Fat! The water is warmer now so I'm swimming more. Evert devised a great exercise. We run up and down the steps of the Roman theater ruins (shown in the postcard that I sent you). That's a different exercise, isn't it?

Thursday, April 9, 1970

Well, today we were treated to lunch at the restaurant by the cook, and guess what he ordered? Fish, one whole one on my plate. I had to eat it, but the funny thing is that it didn't bother me like it used to, despite those eyes staring at me.

Today was a good day. I have days when I'm crazy to see a movie, eat a certain food, drive a car, take a hot bath, or have other "taken for granted" comforts of home. Sometimes I'm bored to death. But I keep realizing that the things that are happening now I'll remember always. And besides, the bored times are few. I do get frustrated for current news, though, and current songs.

I'm having a bikini made by the tailor here. Forty cents for the material and eighty cents for the tailor. Pretty good price, isn't it?

More on the "Süleyman drama." He has now told me that his wife had twins two years ago. She never took care of them. When they were three months old, she dropped them both and they both died. This sounds far-fetched, I know. Whether it's true or not, he believes it's true. He says she is crazy, and from observations, I would agree. I don't know if they have autopsies in Turkey (well, they must, but I don't know if one was done or if they even do them in the village). He said the babies were so little and the event wasn't even questioned by the police. And I guess you aren't allowed to speak out against your wife, so he didn't accuse her publicly. At any rate, he gets so emotional when he talks about it. I really hope for his sake that he can earn the money to leave Turkey and get out of the miserable situation. His family backs him 100 percent. Today his mother brought me a vase of flowers. What a strange, weird world this is. My feelings for him are right now quite strong, but I've felt the same intensity of feelings countless times before for others. What's it called anyway? Puppy love? It's not a permanent love, but I couldn't walk away from it now. I'm enjoying being with an emotional person after my "always the same" ex-husband. It's a beautiful soul thing we have here, but I think I told you before that there couldn't be a future even if I wanted to live in Turkey, because our worlds are impossibly far apart. He just doesn't know where I come from.

Well, I talk and talk. I tell you because I don't tell these things to my friends here. Oh yes, Andrea (the Canadian girl) thinks she's pregnant by the son (Tarik) of the man I told you about who was shown in *National Geographic*. She tried the rhythm method. That's crazy! I think she'll try to get an abortion in Turkey. God! I'll never have that problem. More later.

Love,
Karen

At long last, Bill returned to Side. He and Evert discussed with me again the possibility of my accompanying them to Israel and Egypt. I was very tempted, but the idea of traveling through a war zone finally made me decide against it. Besides, I felt things had eased up now that Süleyman's wife had left the premises for good and all my Turkish friends had convinced me that there was no problem at all in my seeing Süleyman. Evert gave me his address in the Netherlands and encouraged me to visit there when I left Turkey. He was sure I could get a job there through him or his family. That didn't sound like a bad idea; I planned to keep it in mind. Evert planned to return to the Netherlands by early summer; I figured now I'd wait for Helene and Andrea to leave in the next few months.

I haven't mentioned before in detail the clothing of the Turkish village people or, I should say, the amount of it. The women, as I've described before, wore pajamas under two or three dresses and covered their heads with head scarves. The men wore Western-style clothes, although not the latest styles, that were bell-bottoms or flared pants with body shirts. The Turkish pants were a straight-legged baggy-variety made of suit material. Each person owned one or two changes of clothing. I felt "rich," and also embarrassed, with all my clothes, which was only one backpack full. One could recognize a person from a distance by what he was wearing.

Süleyman had two pairs of pants made of gray suit material, one a muted stripe and one a muted plaid. He had one bright red pullover sweater, one beige cardigan sweater, and two short-sleeved shirts, pink and white. He wasn't unusual. This was typical of the village guys. His shoes were falling apart. I could be half a kilometer down the beach and spot a red sweater and gray pants coming my way and know it was Süleyman. None of the Turks appeared to feel a lack; in fact, in all ways that go into a standard of living, these people didn't seem to feel deprived. Muharrem loved his "little house." Süleyman was proud of his two-burner gas range in the pension. When Süleyman made spaghetti (*makarna*), he was excited if his mother had "a little bit of meat" to add to the sauce. A little bit of meat might have been an eighth of a pound for a lot of sauce.

The Turkish attitude toward material things impressed me—and it still does. No one seemed to be striving for "things"; even the people who were "making money" weren't flaunting possessions like they do in the United States. Seeing this and living like this changed me a lot and helped me put a lot of things into a different perspective. Now, away from Turkey, I've easily fallen back into a lot of my old ways, but I doubt I'll ever, and hope I'll never, completely change from the simple ideas and ways of living that I learned in Side.

A couple of days after Evert and Bill left, Süleyman got the idea (and I agreed) that I should move into another pension. Throughout our entire relationship, he had been concerned about the question of adultery; he had always tried to keep us surrounded by people when in the public eye. When we were alone, it was always far from the village. Now that I was alone in his father's pension, he felt that people might wonder what was going on if he went upstairs to visit me. His cousin Halil, who owned one of the restaurants, had a pension also. We decided I should stay there.

Halil's pension was nice and new, and different from most of the other pensions in Side. Instead of being extra rooms in someone's house, it was more like a small hotel. All the rooms were rented out. This pension was almost in the center of town. I could see the coffeehouse from my window. There was a shower for everyone's use with a water heater, and Eastern-style and Western-style toilets. But there was no kitchen. And the price per day was higher than at Süleyman's. Still, I could easily afford it. I felt better being away from Süleyman's family and that whole atmosphere, although I missed everyone too.

CHAPTER 8

Süleyman and I were sitting at Mamadou's restaurant one day when the gendarme commandant (local policeman from Manavgat) came up to our table. Süleyman introduced me. The gendarme then sat down and bought us some small plates of food. He spoke to Süleyman in Turkish for a while. Then he switched to English and told us that Süleyman's wife's family had complained about Süleyman's seeing me. The gendarme wondered about our relationship. We explained to him what was going on, saying that Süleyman had applied for a divorce. The gendarme seemed quite sympathetic to our story. I told him that I was just a tourist and expected to stay for a while longer in Turkey. I didn't want to cause any trouble, but I didn't see anything wrong in being Süleyman's friend when he and his wife were separated, I said. I also explained that when Süleyman and I had become friends, I hadn't even known he was married. I had only been informed of his marital state by Cap a week later when he left Side. The gendarme seemed to completely understand our situation, but he warned us to be careful and not to get caught in a bad position. We assured him that we were very careful and that we certainly didn't intend to get caught doing anything wrong; in fact, we weren't doing anything wrong, we told him.

A few days later, we met again. This time the gendarme bought us dinner. The three of us walked on the beach afterward. The gendarme had gotten quite drunk. I was proud of Süleyman, who appeared sober even though he'd drunk quite a bit of wine. It was the gendarme who was in bad shape that night.

When I related our conversation with the gendarme to Helene, she told me that a few years ago Süleyman had been dating a tourist. Harika's brother, not liking this, one day burst into Süleyman's kitchen and fought with him. For this, the brother spent time in prison. Süleyman and Helene thought that now the brother was seeking revenge for time spent in jail and was initiating the complaints against Süleyman and me.

Day by day, I was learning more and more disturbing things. I truly felt sorry for Süleyman in his position. And I started to regret my involvement with him. But when I'd think of leaving, I'd just look at him and I decide I wouldn't.

He's having so many problems, I thought. *But they'll soon be over and things will be peaceful. It's worth waiting for that.*

I continued meeting some very interesting tourists as they passed through Side. An American woman and her Turkish boyfriend stopped there for a few days. Diane lived in Istanbul and was teaching English. She'd been away from the States for three years, originally having started out as a tourist like I was, and then just staying overseas. I admired her courage. Süleyman and I spent a few evenings in Mamadou's restaurant with them. We all got along well. I realized that often I was imagining a future with Süleyman.

But there were the downsides to our relationship too, besides the problem of Harika's family. Süleyman possessed a jealousy that was intolerable. He was showing this jealousy more and more.

We were in Halil's restaurant one evening. A few other Turkish guys were there. As usual, Turkish music was playing on the record player. Some of the guys began to dance. One of the Turks asked me to dance; I agreed. Süleyman sat there fuming. After a few minutes, he got up and began fighting with the guy. I couldn't believe it; I had danced with other guys before in the restaurants and couldn't see why this time was any different. A couple of the other guys calmed Süleyman down. I walked out of the restaurant, going back to my pension. Süleyman caught up with me. Furious, I asked him what the story was. It appears that Süleyman now understood what platonic relationships between a Western man and woman could be. But he didn't trust another Turk. "They all interested in something," he said. I suppose his close friend

Muharrem, or his cousin Halil, would have been all right, but another Turkish guy wasn't. I found it impossible to persuade him to think differently of the matter. And maybe he was right in a way. So far, I hadn't met one Turk who, after having been friendly, didn't come on to me when we found ourselves alone.

I tried to understand Süleyman and to forget about the incident.

The days I spent in Halil's pension were really good. I began a serious study of Turkish. Instead of just being able to use isolated words, I started being able to speak in sentences. I borrowed Tarik's Turkish-to-English books and tried to formally learn from them, reversing everything. This wasn't always easy, but I had Süleyman to help me. At the same time, I tried to teach Süleyman to write English and to improve his English grammar. Usually about three in the afternoon, after returning from the beach, we'd go sit outside at Mamadou's with a glass of çay and work on our languages.

Also, during this time, we spent more time with Süleyman's Turkish friends from outside Side. Side was a popular place for Turks to come on Sundays. Süleyman was so well liked that his friends from Antalya and other nearby towns would come into Side and ask for him. Then they'd take both of us out for dinner, huge feasts usually. A lot of the conversations would be in Turkish, which I found it helpful, but it was quite frustrating to try to follow what they were saying. But I was slowly improving.

One Sunday, a young rich Turk from Antalya came to Side, bringing his English girlfriend. The English woman was living with the man in his parents' house with complete approval of his parents. She was accepted as a wife would be. This in a country of arranged marriages and enforced virginity before marriage surprised me. Normally village women checked the bedsheets after the wedding night. If they were not bloody, it was grounds for divorce. The Turks seemed to have a double standard for Turkish women and foreign women. I kept seeing examples of how morals in Turkey were different from those I was used to.

Anyway, this couple arrived and bought us a dinner complete with wine. The man got very drunk and then suggested we go for a ride in his new car. Few people owned cars in rural Turkey, so it seemed like a

95

treat. We stopped by Muharrem's and picked up Helene and Muharrem. This man then went roaring through the dirt roads of Side, which seldom see a car. Then he headed out of Side and over to the road that led to the beach, thereafter driving crazily along the beach. Süleyman seemed to think this was great fun; Helene said she was getting carsick; and I was just plain scared. Then the idiot drove his shiny new car into the sea and along the breakers. I really couldn't believe it! Muharrem, the most mature of all the young Turks I had met in Side, ordered the man to drive back on the beach and stop. We all walked back to town. I really think the man thought he had a new toy.

When he was in the village, the gendarme commandant kept inviting us to have çay with him. It seemed to me that he understood exactly what was going on with us and that he approved. Once he suggested that both Süleyman and I leave Side until Süleyman was divorced. I told him that I didn't have the money to keep moving and that I loved Side. I asked if there were any problem with my staying; was there any legal problem in my seeing Süleyman? He assured me that there was no problem. I honestly felt that he just thought it would be easier for the two of us to be together if we left Side—and then we would be able to be alone whenever and wherever we wanted.

Despite the reassurances of everyone I knew, I often had lots of misgivings about staying in Side and threatened to leave a couple of times. When I made those threats, Süleyman would break down and sob and beg me to stay. Turks are very emotional and aren't ashamed of crying or of showing their anger. One day I actually packed, and so did Süleyman. He followed me. We sat waiting for a *dolmuş* outside of town and talked. He finally persuaded me to return.

"All the trouble be finish. Stay, please, please, please, please," he cried. Tears ran down his suntanned face.

Losing my courage and feeling very bad that he was sobbing, I gave up. "Okay, Little Turtle, let's go back to Side. I won't leave," I said, giving up.

So back we went. But I was not at peace with myself.

Once again, I decided to stay in Side through the summer. Helene and Andrea were definitely going to stay. Plus, I had calculated my available money and knew that I couldn't go very far on it. Side was very inexpensive, and I really enjoyed it—and Süleyman too. I again had temporary thoughts of going to the Netherlands and meeting Evert, maybe finding a job there. Süleyman had tales of how great Side became in the summer. Already life was becoming livelier there. Lots more Turkish people would come into town at night and sing and dance at the restaurants, usually to live music. I was really enjoying myself.

But one night, things changed. We were at one of those parties at Dogan's restaurant. Things were going well; we were having a great time. Then Süleyman's father appeared and spoke to his son in Turkish. I couldn't follow what they were saying. Süleyman told me to wait there, saying he'd be right back. But he didn't return. I began to get worried. Helene and Muharrem appeared and said they felt something was going on at the police station. I began to get very uneasy.

After a half hour had passed, Süleyman appeared and told me I was to go with him to the police station. All the way there, I kept asking him what was going on. He insisted that it was nothing, saying that the police just wanted to ask me a few questions. And he was right.

We entered the dimly lit police station. The gendarme and his deputy were sitting on wooden chairs in front of a large desk. They both looked welcoming.

"Why are you in Turkey?" the Gendarme asked.

"I am a tourist."

"How long are you going to stay here?"

"Maybe until the end of summer," I replied.

During the questioning, the police were quite friendly. I left afterward, curious but not frightened.

Halil, Süleyman's cousin, went back to the pension with me. Süleyman said he would come along as soon as he could. But he didn't come. Time went by. From my window in the pension, I could see Harika and her family at the police station, standing around outside. I started to feel tense. The whole thing was kind of nightmarish; I really couldn't understand what was happening. Halil spoke no English. I tried to find out as much as I could from him in Turkish. I guessed he was trying to tell me that Süleyman's wife's family were complaining, mostly because Harika had been locked out of her house.

More time went by and Süleyman still didn't return. The electricity went off at eleven, and Süleyman still hadn't come back. I was getting more and more frightened. Halil suggested we walk to the theater. He wrote a note for Süleyman telling him where we'd be. I was hesitant to leave the room because I didn't want to miss Süleyman, but it felt good just getting outside and walking.

After climbing the theater steps, Halil and I sat at the top and practiced Turkish. He'd say, "*Sen kedi*" (You're a cat), and I'd say, "*Yok, sen kedi*" (No, you're a cat). This went on and on until we became hysterical with laughter. We went through various animals—cow, donkey, dog—and it seemed very funny. Between jokes, we'd talk about Süleyman. Halil kept telling me not to worry. The laughter felt good. I needed it.

When we returned to the room, Süleyman still hadn't appeared. Halil went home. I spent the remainder of the night tossing in bed, worrying and miserable.

The next morning, I awoke early and looked out the window to see if I could see Süleyman anywhere. There was no sign of the gray pants and red sweater.

A while later, there was a knock on my door; a different gendarme was there. I asked him what he wanted, and in slow English he told me that he was requesting me to leave Side. I asked him what in the world that meant—why? The language barrier was too great, so he couldn't explain. I had a good idea, though, that it was something like the gendarme from Manavgat had been explaining: leave to ease the tension in the families.

Feeling shaky and full of tension, I left the pension and walked to the çay house. Süleyman appeared soon after. I told him what had happened. He suggested we look for the gendarme from Manavgat and ask him what was going on. Süleyman said that the previous night, his father had suggested that he not stop and see me, especially since Harika's family was very close to the pension.

Right away, we started making plans. I didn't want to stay in Side any longer, not with this atmosphere. I had felt the troubles were over and I could stay freely as long as I liked; obviously, they weren't over and the whole situation was scaring me too much.

Soon the friendly gendarme appeared. I talked to him. He said the authorities felt that it would be easier if I left. He understood my predicament, and that I felt I was doing nothing wrong, but he thought the divorce or separation would be smoother if I left Side, at least for a few days.

That settled it! Süleyman and I talked, and I decided to go to Istanbul. I had some ideas from having talked to other travelers and I thought that maybe I could find a job there. I was very tired of these troubles in Side. Süleyman decided he wanted to go with me. We went over to Tarik's pension, where the American teacher was staying, and I talked to her about the job she had in Istanbul. She was fantastic and offered to let us stay in her apartment since she was going to be in Side a couple of weeks more. She gave me the address of the institute where she taught and the address of some American friends of hers in Bebek, the suburb where she lived. I felt tremendous relief. Maybe something was going to work out for us after all.

The rest of the day was spent in preparation. I packed, and then Süleyman and I talked to our friends about our plans. Everyone thought it was a good idea to just remove ourselves from Side for a while. Süleyman talked to his father, who said he'd continue working on the divorce while we were gone. Then we would be able to return to Side safely.

That evening, Diane, her boyfriend, Süleyman, and I ate at Mamadou's restaurant and talked about Istanbul. Andrea came over, gave us the address of the boyfriend she'd had in Istanbul, and asked us to get in touch with him. About eleven at night, Diane asked us to go over to Tarik's pension, where they were staying, to pick up her apartment key. Süleyman said that we should all separate and go alone because he was worried that Harika's brother would be after him. It was a terrible, horrifying feeling knowing that there was a possibility that someone with a knife would be after him, or us. I had to admit it was a possibility, though, since it had happened before. I was terrified—

mostly for Süleyman. But we made it. Süleyman had trailed me back to my pension to make sure I got there all right.

This time we made it out of town, taking the minibus to Manavgat and then the bus to Antalya. I felt quite sad, like I was leaving home. The bus for Istanbul was an overnight one, so we had the day in Antalya to sit at çay shops and sidewalk cafes overlooking the sea and to visit Süleyman's friends.

April 19, 1970
Side, Turkey

Dear Family,

How can this be? I'm sitting in a window writing this by moonlight. What next? My gas lamp is broken. I want to get this written tonight if possible.

Dad, you were right in giving me fatherly advice. Please always do that if you feel you should. In this case, you were right—and at least this time I was wary and prepared. Nothing really happened, except that Süleyman began pushing hard for a divorce. The wife refused to leave the property, and things got tense. I changed pensions and began investigating where to go. Tomorrow I leave for Istanbul. An American woman here now has an apartment there. I can stay there until I find some kind of a job. Everyone thinks I should be able to work there. Süleyman is coming with me. His father is going to get him a divorce from Side. Süleyman wants to work in Istanbul.

April 20, 1970
Antalya, Turkey

I gave up on the moonlight. We're in Antalya sitting at an outdoor tea cafe by the sea. It's so beautiful. Antalya is on a bay with mountains rising straight up from the water. It reminds me of places I saw in Switzerland or Norway. There is snow on the mountains and we're here in the sun.

I'm really excited about moving on. And so glad to be traveling in Turkey with a Turk. So I left Side without pictures—also Greece and Yugoslavia. Such is life, I guess. I'm having my mail forwarded to Istanbul.

Your trip, Mom and Dad, sounded so good. Sometimes I'm dying to go back home, but I know there's a lot more I want to do here first.

Oh yes, I got a kidney infection here last week. An American doctor in Side said it is not dangerous if it reoccurs and is very common. I got sulfa pills in Manavgat without a prescription (nice). Three days later, Andrea, the Canadian woman, got it too. Possibly it's bad water.

I'm glad Dad gets his sabbatical. Do you plan to travel from London? If so, where?

I received a really nice letter from Cap's brother. He was worried about my safety in Turkey.

My address in Istanbul will be, Karen, Postrestant, Istanbul, until further notice.

Love,
Karen

CHAPTER 9

The ride to Istanbul was just awful. The bus wasn't that comfortable, and a couple of women just across from us insisted on throwing up the whole time. I couldn't believe it; they would sit there and puke into the *naylon (plastic bag)*, *and then at the next stop, they'd get off and eat. It was hellish; Süleyman said they kept wailing, "I'm going to die; I'm going to die." They were fat, obnoxious, and very noisy. I kept my fingers in my ears the whole ride.*

I continued to be impressed with Süleyman after we got to Istanbul. I'd thought of him as a village guy who didn't know much about getting around outside Side, but I was wrong. He had a sophistication about him that hadn't stood out, particularly in Side. Now in the big city, he fit in perfectly. Not only that, but also compared to Cap, my last traveling companion, he was perfect. I felt spoiled and well taken care of.

The apartment where we stayed was in Bebek, one of the upper-class suburbs of Istanbul. We were very happy to see that place; now we were on our own, all alone, far from Side and the problems. The apartment was in a two-story house, one apartment on each floor. Ours was big, with an enormous balcony that looked out over the River Bosphorus, Flowers were blooming all around, and the whole neighborhood was quite hilly. Inside the apartment, there were two large bedrooms, a living room, and a small kitchen with a two-burner range and a small refrigerator. The bathroom was large, Western style with a tub; water had to be heated separately. I was quite excited because there were some American magazines there and I hadn't seen any for ages. When we sat down, I showed Süleyman pictures of the United States.

Our time in Istanbul was fun. We stayed a little over a week in all. The first day we met Diane's future American roommate, Sandy. Sandy planned to move in a couple of weeks later. She came over to bring some of her things. She was overbearing, big, and fat, and a teacher at the same institute as Diane. Sandy had been in Turkey for a year after having been divorced; I could identify with that. Now she had a Turkish boyfriend too, Mamadou, a student at one of the universities in Istanbul. We were invited over for a spaghetti dinner one night at Mamadou's place where he lived with a bunch of other students.

I did apply for a teaching job at the institute. The woman there was quite receptive and said I definitely qualified for a teaching position. But the problem was that the teaching session had just started. In the fall, they'd need teachers. She said she'd put my name down for that time. Of course, this was only May, which left me with quite a stretch of time to support myself on almost nothing. So I said I'd let her know if I did want the job in September. She was rather discouraging about secretarial jobs in Istanbul for foreigners, as you had to do something that a Turk couldn't do, like teach English. She felt I'd have trouble getting a job anyplace else.

Other than that, Süleyman and I just played in Istanbul. We visited a student who had been on the bus with us who also lived with a bunch of other students in the heart of Istanbul. They fixed us a nice dinner and then took us to a movie.

Another day, Süleyman and I were walking down the highway when a cab driver pulled up beside us. He had visited Side and remembered Süleyman. This called for a reunion celebration, so he took us out for an enormous lunch and drove us all over the suburban sections of Istanbul to sightsee.

We also visited another friend of Süleyman's, one who took his vacations in Side every summer. He, his wife, and their children lived in a suburb across the Bosphorus on the Asian side. We took the ferry over and spent the day with them. After having a delicious meal, we sat and talked. They spoke some English. One of their daughters was quite fluent. I also had a chance to practice my Turkish.

One day we decided to explore Old Stamboul, the old section of the city that contains an incredible concentration of art and architecture.

Our first stop was Topkapi *Sarayı* (the second word meaning "palace"), built in 1450 by Sultan Muharrem II. The palace was extraordinary. It was filled with flower gardens and collections of ancient Chinese porcelain. There were four rooms filled with impressive jewels and a harem—a maze of fourteen halls, terraces, rooms, wings, and apartments grouped around the sultan's private quarters. Everything was opulent and extremely impressive.

We also spent time in the Blue Mosque (the Mosque of Sultan Ahmet). Six minarets surround this mosque. Inside it is decorated with twenty thousand shimmering blue Iznik tiles interspersed with 260 stained glass windows. There is an arabesque pattern painted on the ceiling. It is a beautiful light-filled mosque.

Of course, we mingled with the crowds in the colorful grand bazaar, enjoying the myriad of things to be bought there. That day, I experienced Turkey the way most tourists do, exploring ancient palaces, mosques, markets, and neighborhoods. And I was doing this in a great way, by the side of a Turk, my boyfriend and my guide. The only problem with the day was that I got huge blisters on my feet from all the walking we did.

We also went to a movie downtown, a detective story set in Washington, DC. I had seen it in the States, so I could follow it even though it was dubbed in Turkish. It was fun showing Süleyman where I'd lived before I came to Turkey.

Walt, an American, lived in the upstairs apartment of our building. He came down to visit us sometimes, and we had some good conversations. We also visited him in his apartment; what a great place he had. I wasn't sure, but I gathered he must have been connected with the CIA. He must certainly have been undercover, because he hedged talking about his job or why he was in Turkey.

April 23, 1970
Istanbul, Turkey

Dear Family,

After a really terrible all-night bus ride, we arrived in Istanbul. The suburb we're staying in now reminds me very much of San Francisco. I'm sitting on a balcony now with a view of the water and hills, with green trees and flowers all around. This is Bebek, the expensive section of Istanbul.

Yesterday I went to see about jobs. The semester just started at the teaching institute, but the woman said I could definitely teach English there in the fall (big help). Work permits for office jobs are very hard to get here. Süleyman hasn't looked yet because he's been busy taking me around. And we've been visiting countless friends here of his, always for a huge feast or a movie. At least we've been leading an inexpensive life so far, because the only money we've spent has been for transportation.

Last night we visited student friends of Süleyman's, five guys. They cooked us dinner (ground beef patties, French fries, yogurt, and a pilaf, then honey for dessert). We had a political argument about the Kennedys, with Süleyman as translator (all people here love the Kennedys, it seems).

The Turkish people in Istanbul are really well dressed. Skirts are above the knee, an inch or two longer than mine are. Clothes appear to be quite expensive (seventeen dollars for shoes). I really feel badly dressed. There are so many American cars here; in fact, most of them are old American ones. I don't know—Side and Istanbul are totally different worlds. But I haven't seen a lot of the tourist attractions yet.

The man upstairs just asked me if I wanted to be a governess. That's not what I'm looking for, that's for sure.

Love,
Karen

At last, Süleyman and I were able to live without being harassed by circumstances as we'd been in Side. It was interesting to see how we got along, which was great, except for our physical relationship. Sex had been easy to avoid in Side because we were always afraid someone would come along, but in the apartment, we were alone, and the problem now was evident. He was very rough and hard; I had never known anyone who actually could turn me off by trying to be romantic, that is, if I genuinely liked the person—and I did like Süleyman. I tried to

105

communicate this to him, but he still behaved as if passion must be shown by inflicting pain. Other than that, we got along well and were so busy that the physical problems didn't seem all that important. Little Turtle was a good companion and friend. That's how I thought of him most of the time, and how I still think of him now.

When we weren't eating out with someone, we bought food at the little grocery down the street and cooked at the apartment. I was gaining weight; we ate a great deal of pasta and other starches, always including the inevitable bread. I got very hung up on it, just like the Turks were, sopping up the juices with the bread. It was so good! There was some American cinnamon in the apartment. I tried to fix Süleyman cinnamon toast; it wasn't too successful, toasting the bread over the gas range. Usually he did the cooking. I've never been too great a cook without having a recipe, an oven, and measuring cups.

Our main purpose for coming to Istanbul, though, had been to find jobs. And we hadn't looked very hard. Süleyman hadn't looked at all. I think he'll never work steadily, actually. He's just too lazy. I didn't have much hope of finding any work until the fall. We couldn't stay at the apartment forever. Süleyman felt that if we were to return to Side, the problems might have blown over. Plus, he said he and his father would go into Manavgat the first day and check on the divorce. This would mean that his wife would be helpless in her complaints. I believed this. Why not? Every country's laws are different, and what he said made sense.

Also, both of us were homesick for Side and the lazy life on the beach with our friends. Life in Side was far cheaper. If we'd had to move into our own apartment in Istanbul, life would have been much more expensive than in Side. We could live in Side for almost nothing. Also, it had been warm there for quite a while, whereas the weather still was chilly in Istanbul at times. We longed for the sun and beach. So we decided to return. We were both excited at the prospect, and I had real hope that the problems would be forever ended. It's funny; I didn't want Süleyman to get a divorce so we could get married, as most people would have in that circumstance, probably. I just wanted to stay in Side as a tourist without problems and also wanted to be with Süleyman while I stayed there. Throughout, I continually told him that I would leave at the end of the summer and that there was no permanent future for us. I do think, though, that he hoped for something else. Still, he'd always accept what I said without too much argument. He was sure I'd keep on living in Turkey and that we could build a "little pension" together on his father's land and live happily ever after.

The return trip to Side was much more enjoyable than the trip to Istanbul had been. We traveled during the day, and not one person was sick, even once. The section of Turkey that we traveled through was boring—flat, dry, and barren. It was such a contrast to the mountainous coastline. As we entered Manavgat, banners were flying everywhere and everyone seemed in a festive mood. Then Süleyman realized that it was May 1—May Day. I don't know why, but I was surprised that they celebrated May Day there. This was disappointing, though; it meant that Süleyman and his father couldn't go check on the divorce until Monday.

CHAPTER 10

*S*üleyman and I walked to Side from the far side and made our way to Muharrem's little house. Fortunately, Helene and Muharrem were there, and were surprised and glad to see us. They said talk about us had died down around the village after we'd left and they felt sure there would be no more problems now that we'd returned. It was a beautiful sunny day. I checked into Halil's pension again and headed for the beach. It felt very good to be back.

Diane and her boyfriend were still there. We told them all about our stay in Istanbul. More people had arrived in Side. It's amazing how possessive I felt about that place. I really had adopted it as my home, and it seemed like I knew everyone there.

Monday, Süleyman and his father went to Manavgat to check on the divorce proceedings. When they returned, they assured me that from now on, there'd be no problem. Also, Süleyman talked to his cousin Mamadou, who hired him as a waiter in his restaurant. Süleyman came and went freely to and from Halil's pension and even stayed there with me a few nights. During the day when Süleyman worked, I went to the beach, visited friends, sat around the restaurant, and studied Turkish. The whole routine was great. The only problem was that the restaurant had such long working hours—in at eight in the morning to set up, until eleven at night. All the waiters worked those hours and got miserable pay for it (approximately forty dollars per month). I got quite disgusted with those conditions; it seemed like I never had time with Süleyman and that he was working too hard for almost nothing, constantly running. The restaurant business was picking up with more and more tourists coming, tour buses full of them.

May 5, 1970
Side, Turkey

Dear Family,

I know I'm very late in writing. Just real laziness, I guess.

We're back in Side now. I couldn't find teaching work for the summer. And Süleyman was so sickened by the cost of living in Istanbul (actually cheap compared to the United States, but high for Turkey), so we decided to go back to Side. We missed the close good beach and our friends anyway.

Monday, Süleyman and his father went to a lawyer in Manavgat to start his divorce proceedings. In Turkey, once this is done and the wife receives word of this, there is no problem with the husband's seeing other women. So now there's no legal danger. I'm thankful because the situation was beginning to worry me a lot.

I just got your letters. I promise to write more often. I know how much your letters mean to me.

Mom, your description of the dinner you prepared for your friends made my mouth water. Food in Turkey is delicious, but there's so much not available here. I wish I could see your garden. Your yard in spring is so gorgeous.

Since I've made the big decision to stay here at least until August, I'm wondering how my divorce settlement money should be sent here. Are there any banks there or in Washington that have contact with a bank in Antalya, Turkey? I'll check from here. Would you ask from there? I'll probably be flat broke by then, so I would like the money soon. Thank you in advance.

We spent the day on the beach today as usual and talked to two Englishmen who live on Cyprus. They had diving equipment, and we used it in the really good surf today. I've been trying hard to learn Turkish since we've been back, and I'm learning fast. Somehow I pronounce well, they say. I was so bad in Spanish and French in school, but Turkish is different. I'm also teaching Süleyman to read English and starting to correct his grammar. I was beginning to speak "Turkish-English" and starting to lose my vocabulary because of talking to him and other Turks who don't speak English well.

I don't know about working in Europe. I think I just want to see some new places, relax, and then come back. Don't worry about the lack of decisions. They'll come. And with the exception of a few regrets about the past, I'm happy and enjoying myself.

May 8 , 1970
Side, Turkey

Dear Family,

You asked what people do for a living. Süleyman said, "Tell them I'm a professor-doctor of love." (That's true). Actually, people in Side don't seem to work (the men, that is). They grow food, tend to livestock, and own shops, pensions, hotels and restaurants, but I don't know when the men work, because you see them always sitting around the coffeehouse and beach. The women stay home. They wash, cook, are very busy, and appear content and happy. Süleyman works in his cousin's restaurant when he needs money. And he owns his house.

Everything is so cheap here and one doesn't need much. Life is simple. Everyone has enough to eat and is comfortable, but some Americans might say they're on the poverty level by US standards. But houses are clean, comfortable, and cheerful, and everyone has food and clothing. Süleyman says there are starving people in other parts of Turkey though. Most of the country is rural—farms with lots of fruit.

I think I'll be staying here over summer. It's been a hard decision to make. I'm undecided about my life. The problem isn't that I'm not happy (I am), but I get hung up and think I should be married with kids as is "normal" for American women my age. Other than that, I'm relaxing and enjoying life and meeting new people. There are always new tourists here. Then, too, I do like Süleyman. And now that the wife problem is solved, we're really having a great time. He's a fantastic person, very ignorant about things away from Turkey, like geography and world religions, but he learns so fast and is so interested and has a great psychological understanding of me. Helene and Andrea are also hung up on their Turkish boyfriends here. Such is life, for now. I'm going to Cyprus in ten days to renew my visa for Turkey.

In any case, I'm fine, brown, fat, and happy. I think I needed time away from all the tensions and pressures of US life (and believe me, there are a lot of them that are easy to see when you've been here a while).

Love,
Karen

Despite my sense of safety and well-being, my little "utopia" didn't last long. Harika's family complained again. I had been told that they "couldn't," that everything had been settled. Obviously, the people who had told me this didn't know.

And then things must have been worse than I guessed, because Süleyman decided I should move from Halil's pension into Halil's house. This move was discussed between the two of them. I didn't understand exactly what was going on, as usual. The sense I got was that they wanted to prove to the town and Harika's family that Süleyman and I weren't sleeping together. They probably figured that if I stayed in Halil's house with his family, it was like having chaperones. It all seemed silly to me, but I moved.

Living at Halil's was another experience. Halil lived in a large stone house near the center of town. He was married and had one baby. His wife was the typical village woman, plump, wearing village dress, and sweet. The house had one big room downstairs, which included the kitchen. The floors were stone; there was a little gas range, a small table, and chairs; a few plates and serving dishes were displayed on shelves; and there were embroidered curtains and decorative cloth everywhere. There was no running water; the water was pumped outside and carried in and then poured out through a hole in a concrete bench after use. Upstairs was the living room (my room) with a few formal chairs and a couch, and then Halil and his wife's bedroom. The baby's bed hung from the ceiling in their room. There was a small Turkish toilet outside on the porch. The house reminded me of houses I'd seen in America that had been restored from the pioneer days.

I enjoyed staying there. After Halil closed his restaurant at eleven each night, he and I would go home, his wife would prepare a meal, and we'd all sit and eat by the lantern light. I didn't need the food because I was steadily gaining weight, but it certainly was a treat. I loved the Turkish cooking.

Because of the problems that were going on in Süleyman's family, and also because he didn't like to work much, he quit his job at the restaurant. Actually, I was glad. I didn't care if he was idle or not, and this way I could see more of him. Now the lazy days at the beach began again. Süleyman began to leave the beach at noon to cook for us, and then he would bring a big pan of hot *makarna* (macaroni) and feta cheese, or some other concoction, along with the inevitable bread, back to the beach for us to eat. My size continued to increase rapidly.

More and more tourists were coming to Side now. We met two Englishmen who were soldiers stationed in Cyprus, Ian and Walter. These men told us a lot about Cyprus. Since I had to leave Turkey soon to renew my visa, I was interested to learn all I could. I had thought of going to Cyprus anyway. They highly recommended it and said I wouldn't have a language problem since so many of the Cypriots spoke English. They felt the place was well worth a visit. We listened to radio programs with them broadcast from Cyprus that played current popular songs. Süleyman used their diving equipment too, but since I'm afraid of fish, I didn't try that.

Some travelers in vans came into town. Most were Americans or Europeans. Two vans were owned by couples with children. I admired the couples who were able to travel with their children; one child was a newborn baby. One of the women was single and very obsessed with her German boyfriend. I felt sorry for him because she was so possessive.

Among the new tourists were some Peace Corps personnel. These kids were fluent in Turkish, which impressed Süleyman. One of the men cautioned me and suggested I leave Side; he told me how many American tourists were missing in Turkey and wondered how I dared to stay alone, especially considering Süleyman's marital situation. I felt he was a sheltered baby, overly concerned (hmm, little did I know then).

Feeling I had conquered Süleyman's jealousy, I continued talking to people when I wished to and nothing happened. Süleyman felt that he could trust any Western man. He was convinced that they wouldn't "bother" a woman who was going with someone else. But despite our earlier discussions regarding other men, he still felt quite differently about any other Turkish man. I didn't realize how serious his beliefs were until an episode one night at Halil's.

Halil had come home from his restaurant. He, his wife, and I were eating our late meal. There was a tap at the window, and in came one of the hash dealers of Side, Izmit. He was a particularly good-looking Turk and one whom many of the female tourists liked. All of us sat on the floor. Izmit rolled a huge joint. As they passed it around, I decided to smoke some too, although I hadn't had any for ages.

Suddenly, there was a banging at the window and in stormed Süleyman, screaming at me to come outside. He was furious. Up and down the street we paced as he ranted and raved. It turned out that he'd been spying on me at Halil's because he didn't really trust Halil even though he was his cousin, who was married and his wife was present—and when he saw Izmit enter, he really got upset. The last straw was when he saw me smoking. There wasn't much I could do except explain that I didn't know he'd care if I smoked. And what did it matter? It was my business. There was such a gap between our ideas and us; I was increasingly tired of having to explain the way I felt about what I thought would be obvious to a Westerner.

Meanwhile I made plans to go to Cyprus. Süleyman decided that he'd go with me to Adana to catch the plane since boats didn't begin sailing until June. I was very excited about leaving Turkey for a while and going to another country. Halil's brother was a sergeant in the army in Adana. He contacted him so we could stay at his place.

May 10, 1970
Side, Turkey

Dear Family,

I got the letter you sent to Istanbul in Side. It was forwarded and arrived quickly.

By now, I guess you know that I'm in Side again. Believe me, I've thought for hours and hours about what I should do. It's been a big decision to make. When I was in Istanbul, I decided that the logical thing to do would be exactly what you suggested—go back to the States. I do have a lot of unfinished things to do there.

Well, the trouble was the deadline. I just wasn't ready to go back by May 15. To be honest, part of the reason was Süleyman. I just couldn't imagine leaving and never seeing him again. At this point, I truthfully am hung up on him right now. Knowing my romantic history, this will probably pass, but there are times when I feel I love him. Maybe it's the novelty of a foreign man. I think I told you before that Helene and Andrea are similarly hung up on Muharrem and Tarik.

But there are other reasons I'm going to stay. I would arrive in the United States virtually penniless. I'd have to work to get money just to get to Illinois and see you, and then probably work in Illinois to get money to get settled in California (or someplace warm). If I stay here, it will cost me another $200 and almost nothing more—maybe $60–$70 to live, and I'll have a free summer on the sea. Yes, I'm lazy. I know it. I always have been.

I really appreciate your advice and your trying to help me from so far away. I know very well I've been causing you many headaches and worries in the last few months, and I'm really sorry. I think I probably won't try to work in Europe. I tried Istanbul, and I'm spoiled enough to want to live better in a big city than I could in Europe as I am. I'd want a car, all my clothes, and a warm climate. California is the place, I think, for when I go back.

Süleyman and I go to Adana, Turkey, in a week, and I'll fly to Cyprus from there for two to three days.

More and more tourists are coming here all the time. It's in the high eighties, always sunny and clear. Wish you were here.

May 18, 1970
Side, Turkey

Dear Family,

I'm listening to love songs in English from Cyprus today and it's making me miss all of you especially. It seems like so long since I've heard from you.

I've been making plans today, and they're fairly well set now. Wednesday I'm taking a bus from Manavgat to Adana (a Turkish city on the coast east of Side). It's an all-day ride along the coast. From there, Süleyman's cousin who lives there will meet me, and I will stay at his house overnight. Then he'll take me to the Adana airport and I'll fly to Cyprus. I wanted to take a boat, but they don't begin sailing until June. My visa for Turkey ends the day I fly.

This will be my first move completely alone, but it's a good place to start since they speak English in Cyprus. I know I won't be lonely long—there are so many people traveling now. I hope I can stay in a youth hostel there. Anyway, my plans are now to come back to Side. I'll probably wait until June when the boats are running. If I'll be there long enough, I'll send you an address there. Otherwise, please write to Side. I'll get it when I get back.

Life in Side is picking up. More and more people are coming. Some Americans just came, married, traveling with babies and children, and camping in VW campers. It's really cool, I think. We spent some fun evenings listening to their music on portable tape recorders and talking about home. It's so good to talk to them. I admire people like that who are mobile and out of the day-to-day rut, like I was in when I lived in Washington.

Also, I moved out of my pension into Süleyman's cousin's own home (Halil). He is married and has a baby. This was done so everyone would know positively that I am not sleeping with Süleyman while this divorce thing is going on. This Turkish village home reminds me of homes in Williamsburg inside. So basic. There are handmade crocheted or embroidered things everywhere. The baby's bed hangs from the ceiling. There is no running water. The floors are rough wood. A two-burner gas range sits on a stone on the floor. So unreal.

What to say? Well, I'll describe some food here. Zucchini stuffed with rice mixture, tomatoes and grape leaves, also stuffed; a pastry rolled and stuffed with cheese. Fantastic salads (tomatoes, cucumbers, lettuce, onions, all chopped with oil and lemon dressing). Really good soup of all kinds. Tonight we had lentil soup with croutons on top. I told them I put croutons on salads, and they were really shocked. I've been reading mystery novels (so-so) that I borrowed. Hope to buy some good books in Cyprus.

Again, I miss you all very much and am anxiously waiting for your next letter.

So write soon, and I'll write right away from Cyprus. Don't worry about me. I'm fine.

Love,
Karen

The day came when Süleyman and I were to leave for Adana. That morning I was in for a rude awakening. I heard some yelling, and then Harika came storming into my bedroom. I was very scared. She yelled at me in Turkish; most of it I couldn't understand. But I knew she was telling me to leave Side. I tried to tell her I was leaving that very day, to Cyprus, but I didn't know the Turkish word for "Cyprus," so she didn't understand me. This was the first time she'd ever spoken to me except to smile and say "*merhaba*," so this was a shock. I also told Harika that Süleyman was just my friend. I could see Halil's wife in the doorway, obviously very upset.

"Today, today—I go to Cyprus," I kept saying to her in Turkish. "I don't want Süleyman." I knew enough Turkish to say these things, and I repeated them. I'm sure she didn't know what "Cyprus" meant, but she did know I would be leaving and seemed satisfied. She left. I was a shaking, quivering mass! What in the hell was going on?

I have to say that all through this situation, I felt in the right. If I had been in the United States and had been seeing a man who was married but separated and who had filed for divorce, I would have felt that this was all right. I didn't cause the marriage breakup or the other problems, and I wasn't openly or publicly doing anything illegal. Besides, I didn't want to marry Harika's husband, as I had repeatedly told him. But Turkey wasn't the United States, and the morals, values, and laws were very different. I just didn't understand how different.

Very soon after Harika left, Süleyman came by to pick me up. I immediately told him what had happened, and he was very understandably upset. He promised me that when I returned from Cyprus, there would be no more problems. I began taking his predictions with a grain of salt, but I still felt there was no real danger to me.

CHAPTER 11

*S*üleyman and I took the minibus to Manavgat and then caught the bus to Antalya. There, Süleyman went through a series of maneuvers to get us a minibus ride to Adana. This minibus was going to be for us only; he had decided we'd travel in luxury this time—the two of us with a driver. Finally, he found a driver who was going to leave in the late afternoon. We spent the day in çay shops and visiting Süleyman's friends, waiting.

The ride to Adana wasn't bad at all. The coastline of Turkey is gorgeous and mountainous with beautiful views of the turquoise sea below. The road was winding. The driver told us that he'd been sick on his first few trips until he got used to it. I was glad he'd gotten used to it; the ride in the small bus with the three of us was much more comfortable than a ride on a bigger bus would have been with people getting sick, most likely.

We arrived in Adana in the early evening and took a taxi to Halil's brother's home. Saban was a slightly built Turk with a light complexion who really resembled his brother, Halil. Süleyman explained the situation to him, after which Saban directed us to a hotel to stay for the night and also set up a time for us to meet the next day. He thought he could find a free place for us to stay in the army living quarters for the next night. Evidently, there was no extra room in his own house. Halil had thought there would be.

The hotel was not very nice, but it was the right price. We met Saban the next day at his office. He took us to the bachelors' enlisted quarters of the army and gave us a room. We then set out to the Türk Hava Yollari Office to make reservations for me. Here we had bad news;

there were only flights twice a week to Cyprus, and the next day's flight was booked with students returning to Cyprus for vacation. This meant a wait of three days. Meanwhile, my visa was going to expire. I made a reservation for the next open flight and headed for the American Consulate to ask what I could do about an expired Turkish visa.

It seemed strange to walk into the American Consulate. Everything looked very luxurious, and "American," of course. I showed Süleyman the US flag and pointed out places on the map that I'd told him about. One of the consular officers saw me in his office and made a few phone calls; he assured me that it would be all right for me to stay the extra three days in Turkey. I wouldn't have to worry about a fine. The man was really nice and quite interested in the fact that I was staying so long in Turkey and traveling by myself to Cyprus.

The three days in Adana were hell. First, Adana isn't on the sea. It would have cost us quite a bit to take a bus to the coast. It was boiling hot, and there just was no way to cool off. I was continually thirsty. Also, because of the horseshit on the streets from the horse-drawn taxis, the place really stunk! And there seemed to be nothing at all to do.

One day, we were sitting in an outdoor café, roasting, and a fat middle-aged Turk came up to us. He and Süleyman became quite friendly and he began treating us to tea. Soon, we were on our way to a restaurant. We had the fanciest, most elaborate meal I'd had in Turkey, complete with wine. This kind of meal is called a meze and is composed of numerous appetizers. It starts out with maybe two or three small dishes on the table, and then slowly, slowly, more dishes are added. I couldn't believe it; the plates just kept coming and I just kept eating. Altogether, we ended up with what would have been quite a few normal-sized meals apiece. I got a taste of many typical Turkish dishes. It was really impressive and delicious. But near the end of the meal, the Turk offered to buy me some dresses the next day, which made both me and Süleyman suspicious. Süleyman politely refused. He certainly had a knack for making friends and being treated by them, even if sometimes those people had ulterior motives.

Most of the time in Adana, I was very bored. Süleyman found some guys in the barracks who played cards. He spent lots of time doing that. And he insisted that I sit there beside him and watch him. I wasn't very interested since I didn't understand the game they were playing. Besides, I was frustrated by the Turkish, not being able to understand all of what they were saying. Sometimes I think it's easier not to know one word of a language than to know some and be constantly straining to understand it all.

I found some of the soldiers frightening; they were constantly staring at me. But what did I expect staying in a soldiers' barracks? Nevertheless, I didn't enjoy their stares. One night, I got a real scare. I walked into the women's restroom and into a stall. I couldn't lock the door of the stall. The next second, the door was pushed open and in walked a Turk, the one who had been standing guard on our floor. I screamed at him and hit him. He ran out of the building. Immediately, I ran into our room and told Süleyman, who then told some of the other soldiers. I guess that man got into some trouble. After that, I made even more of a point never to catch anyone's eye. Obviously, I had encouraged him when I spoke to him in passing.

One night, we watched a movie on the balcony. Lots of the career soldiers and their wives and families attended. I was struck by how differently the women were dressed, like the women in Istanbul, all of them in Western clothing. I had once thought that the village dress was the way all Turkish women dressed, but I had been wrong.

My plane to Cyprus left late in the afternoon of the third day. Süleyman took me to the airport on the airport bus. Saban met us there, and it's a good thing he did, because I had trouble with my expired visa. Obviously, the American Consulate didn't have much pull after all, because the airport guard there tried to fine me for staying over those three days. Magically, Saban took care of it somehow (Süleyman said he knew the particular guard). So I made it out of Turkey—and took off for Cyprus, my first trip completely alone.

This little trip to Adana further reinforced my feelings that my relationship with Süleyman was a thing of the present and definitely not for the future. I was often irritated and bored by him, and I felt a rush of relief when the plane took off for Cyprus.

On the plane, I sat by an American man named Don, a businessman who lived in Istanbul. He was quite friendly and said that he often made trips to Cyprus. He recommended a hotel to me, saying that they had good rates and the place was well located in Nicosia, the capital. I had planned to stay in a youth hostel but decided to have a look at this hotel first.

My first view of Cyprus from the air disappointed me. All I could see was brown flat land. Obviously I had missed the mountains on the coast and was just looking at the flat land in the center of the island. I felt dread; why was I coming to this ugly place? When we landed, I had an even different impression. The city was on flat land but was surrounded by mountains. There were a great many cars and a big four-lane highway leading into town. This was such a contrast to anything I'd seen in Turkey.

Don paid for the taxi into town. We went right to the Carlton Hotel that he'd spoken about. What a modern place Nicosia was. It was another world. There were new sports cars everywhere and modern white buildings. People were dressed in the latest fashion. I hadn't seen anything like this for months. It seemed very strange.

Don's friend who owned the Carlton said he had no vacancies for that night. I was ready to leave, but Don insisted I stay until he called another friend, an American who worked for the embassy, John Wagner. I didn't see what good that would do, but I agreed to wait. Besides, we were going to have cold drinks and snacks and I was hungry.

John Wagner arrived. He was in his twenties, was rather plain and slender, and seemed very nice. He insisted that we go to his apartment and spend the night there. Then we could see if the Carlton would have vacancies for the next night. I decided there was safety in numbers; besides, these men seemed very respectable and I was enjoying the chance to talk to Americans again. So I agreed.

And I found luxury! What a treat it was. I got my own bedroom in a beautiful apartment, which seemed opulent after my Turkish pension. John had a stereo and other "American essentials," but these were things I hadn't seen for a while, so everything seemed incredible. John seemed to be a millionaire. There was running hot water in the bathroom. John had a refrigerator. How fast and easily one can adjust to another environment and take it for granted. I had forgotten my previous "essentials" in just four months. And what was even stranger is that I found the things in John's apartment to be unnecessary and extravagant. Did people need to live like this? Well, I always had, but I had just recently and very quickly learned to live a much more simple life, not only accepting it but also enjoying it.

John and Don took me out to have pizza at Jack's Pizza House that night. I had a Coke in a glass with ice (I never did believe the Turkish idea that drinking a hot beverage would cool you off); I still have a passion for cold drinks with lots of ice. The pizza was a treat too. It seemed strange to be having my old favorites again.

After the pizza, we went to a cabaret to see some Lebanese belly dancers. The next stop was Skorpios Discotheque. All this was a bit overwhelming. I experienced a mild case of culture shock, I'm sure. Those men treated me like a queen, truly spoiling me.

The next day, Don called the Carlton and there were vacancies. Don and John both talked to me and said they thought I should stay at John's even so. There was the extra room, and I would save money. It was a tempting deal, as I had hoped to meet people, and here I had. The vibes were good between John and me; I knew he'd give me no trouble. I had no interest in becoming involved with him, and he was the type that wouldn't bother me if I didn't want him to. So I accepted the invitation—why not? I was having a good time. Plus, this seemed like it would be a good way to see Cyprus, with someone who lived there.

I had a great week. John worked at the embassy during the day. Don stayed in Cyprus for a few more days. On one of those days, I went with him to his office and did some typing. Don worked for a US moving van company that was currently trying to get the navy account. He also had dinner with us a few times; we had some great meals—Chinese food at the Pagoda, a huge meze at a Greek Cypriot restaurant. We went to another cabaret, where we saw flamenco dancing, among other things, and also one of the most obscene dances I'd ever seen, done with a feather. During the day, I'd lie on the roof in the sun, write letters, do shopping, and run errands.

When John had an afternoon off, he and Don took me to Kyrenia, a beautiful small village on the north coast. To get there we had to cross the Green Line, the political division of the Turkish sector and the Greek sector of Cyprus.

Kyrenia has a small horseshoe-shaped harbor and a picturesque ancient castle. We took a tour of the area and then headed to the beach on the eastern side of Kyrenia, Snake Island. John and Don, neither sun lovers nor swimmers, sat the whole time up in the restaurant watching. I swam a lot and decided to swim out to the island. A guy who had been watching me decided to do the same. We met at the island. He was a Scot, stationed with the UN Forces on the island. He was tall, tan, and quite handsome, and had a thick British accent that I found hard to understand. We talked and walked round the island until my feet got cut on the scrubby growth and rocks. He ended up carrying me down. After he'd asked if he could take me out, I explained my situation, saying that I was visiting John but wasn't involved with him. Still, I felt I should spend my evenings with him since he always planned something for me. The guy understood and suggested that he take me to lunch the next day instead. I agreed, thinking John would be working then. He then went up with me to the restaurant, where he met John and Don.

The next day I was almost ready for the Scot to come by to pick me up when in walked John. I just didn't know what to say; he'd gotten the afternoon off and wanted to take me to lunch. I panicked and decided not to tell him the other guy was coming by. We walked out of the apartment probably minutes before the Scot arrived. The Carlton Hotel was very near to the apartment, just around the corner. We went there to pick up Don. From the hotel window, I could see the Scot walking up and down the street, probably looking for a street number. I felt terrible and didn't know what to do; stupidly I decided just to stay there and hide. Looking back at some of these things now, I just think, *What an ass I was.*

Later that afternoon, Don and I were doing errands downtown—and who came up to me? The Scot. He acted rather snotty and sarcastic, but he did say he'd been sorry to miss me. I was very embarrassed and ashamed.

The most important thing I learned from this episode was that despite what I continued to feel for Süleyman, I could easily forget him, be fickle, and change my mind. I wasn't ready to be attached to anyone yet.

During the week I was in Nicosia, John and other Americans I met kept suggesting I get a job in Nicosia. I had told them I wanted to work somewhere in the Middle East so I could stay overseas. These people were sure I could get a job and were very encouraging. John took me to talk to some Cypriot friends of his. One of them was Jack at the Pizza House. Jack was positive he could help me find a position, saying that anytime I was ready we could begin job hunting. I explained that I had to return to Turkey to get my things, saying that I would be back sometime during the summer. The manager at the Carlton was helpful too, positive that I would be able to find work and promising to help me. Also, John saw an ad in the Nicosia paper indicating that the British Embassy was looking for a secretary. One morning, I took a taxi to the embassy and talked to the man in charge of hiring. The position had just been filled, but we had a long talk. He, also, was encouraging about my prospects for finding a job. I became increasingly excited about the idea of working in Cyprus. It was a foreign country, beautiful and culturally interesting, but it also had Western qualities that I liked. It seemed to me a combination of a great many good things.

John took me to an American Embassy party one night, a potluck dinner. I feasted on all the American-style cooking, like macaroni and cheese, hot dogs and beans, and potato salad. While I was there, a tall, creepy guy became quite interested in me and tried to convince me to go out with him. I explained that I was with John, saying that, besides, I was leaving the next day to go to Turkey. Somewhere during the conversation, I told him I'd be coming back to Cyprus. He gave me his name, address, and phone number so I could contact him when I came back if I needed help. Another friend of John's gave me the same information. John said I could stay with his friend when I came back while I was looking for a place to stay. John was due to leave Cyprus in a month so wouldn't be there when I returned.

My last day in Cyprus, I received a letter from Süleyman. Although Helene told me Süleyman had dictated it to her, she had obviously corrected his English as she wrote.

May 30, 1970

Dear *Sevgilim (Darling),*

This is Süleyman speaking, Helene's handwriting. (He just corrected my spelling.)

I miss you like crazy too. I can't stand Side without you. In fact, no one sees me at the beach anymore. Well, I hope you don't work, and come back as soon as possible.

Last night I went to the discotheque (alone). Changed records all night and watched everyone else dancing. I have hardly slept since you left.

You asked about my trip. The bus arrived, plodding along, in Manavgat at four in the morning. Little Turtle walked to Side in the moonlight, talking to himself. During the return (Adana–Manavgat) as I began to doze off, a rabbit jumped in front of the bus. Everyone stood up to see, and I, half asleep, grabbed the man (mute) beside me, saying, "Karen. Did you see the rabbit?"

Side is still quiet; everyone is still enjoying their little quarrels; Chantal and Veronique have found two willing men; and everyone is satisfied.

Yes, ask about work for me in Cyprus. I am interested, of course. Don't forget to mention I speak Greek.

My wife is still living in my house and the divorce papers are very slow in coming through. No one seems to know when they will, but my father is working on it.

The weather is great and the beach tempting, but no fun without you.

Ben seni çok seviyorum! (I love you!)

Hi, This is Helene speaking now. I'm afraid the letter doesn't sound much like Süleyman, but how can I record his beautiful fractured English?

Oh God, stop it! I'm jealous, but I sure am glad that you have found such a lush setup in Cyprus. Trust, Karen!

Süleyman has been moping about, drinking at night and hiding at home. The first word on his lips is always *Karen*. He really misses you, but the situation hasn't cleared up at all. Everyone is really quiet now and there are no exterior problems, but nothing is moving. That's Turkey.

Even if your friends aren't exactly poets, hell, live it up for a while. You can use the safety release, *n'est-ce pas?*

You must see our "new apartment" when you return. We've been redoing Muharrem's little house. Efficiency and roominess.

Muharrem says hello. We all hope you enjoy your stay in Cyprus and return when you feel the time is right.

Helene

All in all, it was a great week. John couldn't have been nicer to me in any way, and he showed me a lot. He was helpful and considerate and never bothered me. The whole thing couldn't have been better.

But I was anxious to return to Turkey. I missed Süleyman, and I had thought of the idea of maybe his going to Cyprus and getting work on the Turkish side. I hadn't seriously put my thoughts together, but I liked the idea because I thought it would be fun to have him around and also because I thought it would be really good for him to leave Turkey. Here I was still using my American values, thinking he would be better off with a higher standard of living, meaning more material things, and having a "good" job. I can see now—actually, it became clear to me within a year probably—that he was perfectly happy in Side. He worked when he wanted and when he needed something, and there wasn't the pressure to have "things," many of which aren't important at all. And they're even less important when the people around you don't have them either and don't care or even know they exist. Still, another reason I thought of his going to Cyprus was to get him out of his awful marriage situation.

Then on Saturday, John took me to the airport. Since he worked at the embassy, he had a pass to go through customs even though he wasn't leaving the country. So he took me through. And then we said goodbye.

May 24, 1970
Nicosia, Cyprus

Dear Family,

Thanks for the fast, good letter.

Today, I'm in Nicosia, Cyprus. I arrived here yesterday from Adana, Turkey. I've really had luck. I sat by an American businessman who works in Istanbul. He introduced me to a young single American man who works for the embassy here. Coincidentally, he lived one block from me in Falls Church. So we're staying in his apartment free, which is good, because Cyprus is expensive. It's a "no strings attached" deal (I have my own room), and that's good because I'm hung up on Süleyman and I don't want to have to hassle with anyone about sex. John treats me like a queen and hasn't even attempted to hold my hand. He's really just a nice man. I also think he's enjoying having an American woman around since there's a problem in dating Greek girls here. One date and they're considered engaged. Anyway, these people are showing me around and say they can easily get me a good job here if I want it.

Cyprus is so different from Turkey. It's very modern. The population is Greek, Turkish, and English, and the Greeks and Turks hate each other and live in separate quarters. I haven't seen the Turkish quarters yet. Everyone speaks English, and American products are everywhere. Nicosia is in the middle of the island, about a twenty-minute drive from the coast. I think the population is about one hundred thousand. There are mountains all around the edge of the island. The climate is mild; it snowed once last winter, which was unusual, they say. I've been eating hamburgers and corn flakes and drinking iced Cokes, a big treat after four months. Last night we went to two fancy nightclubs where they had belly dancers and other dancers from the Middle East white slave market.

The cost of living here is more than in Turkey, but so is the pay and the standard of living. John's apartment is in a new building. It has two bedrooms, a big kitchen, a living room, a dining alcove, and walnut built-in fixtures. He's paying $70/month with no utilities. He has a maid one afternoon a week ($2.40). His apartment is close in quality to my old one in Virginia, minus air-conditioning, dishwasher, and disposal. I've been told I could make £70–£100 per month to start here as a secretary (£1 = $2.40). That's very low for the United States, but good for here. I could buy a car, have a nice apartment, live well, and save some. Another thing: they take "siestas" here for two hours in the afternoon, which is perfect for a sun lover like me.

When I came here, it was to see Cyprus and renew my Turkish visa. But I've been talking to so many people and things are beginning to fall into place. I really wanted to stay over here longer, but I didn't want to work in Europe (too cold). And Cyprus really seems to be ideal. And it's well located for travel to places I haven't seen yet.

These plans of course are tentative, but I want you to know what I'm thinking about. I think I'll return to Turkey this weekend via Adana. Süleyman's cousin will meet me and put me on a bus to Manavgat. I'll stay in Side until the middle of July. Meanwhile, I'll write to the man here who will arrange a temporary job that will then enable him to get me a work permit and job.

Süleyman is such a little doll! He just beamed when I showed him the "Hi, Süleyman" that you wrote. He's so interested in my family and he always wants to say hello to you or write something. The love is such a pure, sweet thing that I'd be happy to hold onto it if only there were some way for us to make it financially somewhere. But if I took him to America, what could he do? And could I be happy with what he could do?

Basic living is cheap, but anything at all luxurious is far more expensive than in the United States, and the people work much longer hours for much less money. Süleyman is intelligent and learns fast, but he doesn't have much formal education because only the rich go to college in Turkey.

These American people I'm with now are driving me crazy in a way. They're helping me, but I'd rather talk to Süleyman and my Turkish friends any day than to these people. They use atrocious English words like *ain't*, and double negatives. I can picture them in front of Saturday afternoon TV drinking beer. But they think they're VIPs. And they have this superior attitude about the countries they've visited. Oh well.

God, I sound like such a snob. I guess I am, and an ungrateful one at that.

Süleyman went with me to Adana. God, I'm glad he did, because I couldn't fly on Thursday (as I had planned) and had to wait until Saturday. Adana is dirty and terrible. I would have gone crazy there alone. It's not on the sea either. Süleyman's cousin is a noncommissioned officer there, so we stayed cheaply in the NCO club.

Right now, I feel like I'm back in the United States. I'm at a US Navy and Embassy baseball game and am writing this letter at the same time. The embassy world is Little America in a way. Tonight a bunch of us are going to a discotheque with a live band. I haven't heard one for four months. Ugh! The screaming and cheering is driving me crazy. My ears are conditioned to Side's quiet.

I saw the *Life magazine spread on Turkey in the US Consulate in Adana. Those mountains and springs are near Izmir, a day by bus from Side. If I can stand the thought of another bus ride (crowded, hot, long) in Turkey, Süleyman and I will go take a look this summer. The ride to Adana was beautiful, along the south coast of Turkey. We saw village women carrying huge loads of wood on their backs, a lot of camels, gorgeous blue sea.*

127

I expect to be back in Side in two weeks, so write either here or there and I'll have mail forwarded from this address: Karen, c/o American Express, Nicosia, Cyprus.

Life is strange, isn't it? A year ago, I never would have believed I'd be writing this letter today. But here I am, and I feel surprisingly happy and strong.

The one drawback to these plans is not being able to see you. I would have stayed longer with you in January if I'd known this might happen. I miss all of you and wish we could talk in person, but your letters are so good and I get so excited when I see one waiting for me.

I'm really tired, so I will stop for now. John will mail this from the embassy, so it should get there faster than from Turkey. Write your candid advice soon.

Love,
Karen

At the Adana airport, after I'd checked through customs, I was waiting in the airport lounge for the flight to arrive and I had the surprise of my life. Up walked Ian, the English soldier I'd met in Side. He couldn't believe I was there either. And he was going to Side.

We sat together on the flight. I told him about my plans; he agreed that Cyprus would be a great place to live and work. He also thought Süleyman would enjoy going there. Ian was quite fond of Süleyman.

Saban met the plane as we'd planned. I tried to introduce Ian to Saban, and I do think Saban was confused. I explained that Ian was a friend of Süleyman's too, but I imagine he was wondering just what I was doing with another man. Anyway, we all got into a taxi, and then Saban found us a hotel. Here again, things were weird; Saban discussed the situation with the hotel manager and the man showed us to a large room, one with three beds. Ian and I looked at each other in surprise; we certainly hadn't intended to stay together. But Saban insisted this was the cheapest way. I told Saban that the accommodation was all right, but I said that we didn't want anyone else in the room, that it should be just for two people. Saban discussed that with the hotel manager, and then the matter was settled. Then Saban told us goodbye, wished us a good journey, and told us to tell all his relatives hello in Side. I hardly knew Ian, and here I was going to spend the night in the same room with him. I was more than uncomfortable.

Ian and I had a good laugh about the situation after Saban left. The hotel was pretty foul; the toilet room was ghastly and stunk to high heaven. Ian and I, after deciding to go out to eat, found a nice restaurant where we had kebabs and salad. Then since we both had a craving for ice cream, we bought cones. Turkish ice cream is sticky stuff, very unlike our ice cream, but I loved it and wanted it whenever I saw it. Ice cream wasn't available in Side, so whenever Süleyman and I went to Manavgat or Antalya, we had to buy a big dish of it for me.

Ian and I went back to the hotel and had a long talk about his life. I found out he'd been married and divorced just recently. His wife had had an affair with an African man. Ian was still quite upset about the whole thing. We talked about Süleyman. Ian seemed to feel that he and I had a "good thing" and that there could be some future in it, the very idea I'd kept dismissing. I told him my doubts about our future. He felt that in Cyprus, there could be a good combination of the cultures. I still felt privately that I wouldn't mind at all if Süleyman went to Cyprus, but I still knew our relationship couldn't be permanent. But Ian was the first Western person who took our relationship seriously.

When it came time to go to bed, we both got into our separate beds in our underwear. Here was another example in my life—all gained from this trip—that it is possible to sleep with a man without having to fight him off constantly. It was a good feeling. John and Ian were men who either felt as I did or else respected my platonic feelings about them.

Early the next morning, the hotel manager knocked on our door since we had to catch the first bus to Manavgat. Ian and I sat in a little çay shop downstairs and were stared at constantly. I was the only woman around, as usual. The bus ride was very enjoyable. I found myself being quite excited at the prospect of returning to Side and seeing Süleyman again. When we arrived at Manavgat, we found a minibus right away.

Yes, I could leave Turkey, leave Süleyman behind, and hardly miss him, but then I could hardly wait to see him when I returned. What was this relationship to me anyway?

CHAPTER 12

The minibus parked right in front of the *çay* shop in Side. Ian and I both climbed out. The first person I saw was Halil, who greeted me quite affectionately and told me that Süleyman was in his restaurant. I ran to the restaurant and went inside. There he was, looking great. It seemed strange, because even though I'd been away just a week, he looked a little different. Still, he looked wonderful!

We were both excited and happy to see each other again. I gave Süleyman the blue shirt I'd bought him in Nicosia. It suited him perfectly. We also sold the American cigarettes and scotch I'd brought back at a great profit; they're very expensive in Turkey.

Things were fine in Side, Süleyman said. He'd arranged for me to stay at his brother's house. Saying that Ali wanted me to stay there, he thought he might stay there with me himself.

So we went to his brother's. Ali was a friendly guy who was married and had two little girls, Ayla and Pembe. They showed me to my room, which was nice and furnished in typical Turkish village style. The house was small with two bedrooms, a living room, a kitchen, and a Turkish-style toilet. I loved it; it was meticulously clean and faced the sea. They had a garden in back and lots of land. Such a simple, happy life they were living, I thought.

Süleyman and I spent the first night there together. But the second night, we decided that it probably wasn't wise at all. After that, Süleyman slept at his father's, as he had before. Ali's wife served good meals, filling and delicious. We conversed as well as possible in my limited Turkish.

The first day I was back, I sat down and wrote the following letter to my parents, telling them my plans and asking them if they'd please lend me some money to help me get to Cyprus, seeing as I wouldn't get my divorce settlement from Dick until August. Excited about going back to Cyprus, I told Süleyman all about my plans. He was positive he wanted to go along too. Even Helene and Muharrem were interested in going. Muharrem's tomato crop wasn't doing that well that summer; eventually he and Helene wanted to leave Turkey and go to Germany to work. Working in Cyprus would enable them to make enough money to get to Germany. So all of us were excited.

June 1, 1970
Side, Turkey

Dear Family,

I'm back in Side temporarily. I really had a good time in Cyprus, squired around constantly by my American friends. I feel like I know a lot about Nicosia.

I've finally decided on my future for the next months. I love Cyprus and I can definitely work there, thanks to the contacts I made while there. I will stay here in Side until I get things straightened out to leave, probably at the end of June.

It would take pages to try to explain why I've decided to stay overseas longer and work. There are many reasons: (1) I want to travel more here and need more money to do so; (2) I like living in a foreign place; (3) I don't want to face the obnoxious singles dating thing in the States. Mainly though, it's just a feeling that has been developing as I've been here—and I have been trying to figure out what happened and why, and where I go from here. I'm tired of the rush and pressures of America. Can you understand my feelings? I hate not being able to talk to you in person.

Cyprus is foreign with lots of different nationalities living there. It's centrally located for travel, it's a beautiful island; and I can work there using English. I really want to try it for a while.

I'm sick of money problems, and I'm anxious to get to Cyprus and begin working and saving again. Would it be possible to borrow money from you (or have you take out a bank loan for me) until my car from the marriage is sold and I receive the $800 in August? I'm tired of the problem of handling things through you, but I don't know how else to do it. I think $300 would be enough to get me to Cyprus and settled in an apartment until I get my first paycheck. Right now, I have about $80 and it's not enough. What I would like to do is have the $300 sent here and have Dick send the money he owes me (car money, $800, bond) to you. That way you could pay yourself back the $300 and send the rest to me in Cyprus. Does this sound reasonable to you? I was told that it would be best to send me money to Turkey in the form of a $300 bank draft. Then I can take it to a bank here and get my money.

As I said before, I hate asking you these favors, and I wish I'd planned this out before I left the States. But life is unpredictable, and so am I.

I have American friends in the embassy there who can receive packages for me in Cyprus duty-free (through the FPO address). I'll write to Dick and ask him to please pack my good clothes and send them that way, so I'll have clothes to work in (surface air mail should take about week, they say).

Please let me know immediately about the money, because I'm anxious to leave and start working. I've been sitting on beaches and thinking about my life long enough now. I've met so many Americans over here who have done as I have done, that is, leave for a vacation in Europe, get hung up, and stay much longer. I'm not the only weird one. I was kind of floundering around until I got to Cyprus and fell in love with it.

Naturally, this means I will leave Süleyman again, and I don't like to. But I can't live forever on savings. It's just a big problem. Enclosed is a picture of the two of us (God, I look fat!).

I'll write more later in detail about my plans, but I wanted to get this plea for a loan off right away. I'm writing to Dick right now to beg him to work out some financial thing with you. I would hope the sale of the car would cover the $300 you send me so you wouldn't be short of cash long.

Anyway, please let me know right away so I can plan further. If I can't get the money, I'll have to stay in Side until I receive the $800 from Dick in August. And I don't want to do that.

Thank you in advance for your help and understanding. I miss all of you very much.

Love,
Karen

The next few days were relaxed and wonderful. It was very good to be back in Side. I was determined to relax (but what else could you do in Side?) before I began working in Cyprus. Every day was beautiful and sunny just like it had been since March. We sat on the beach, and in the restaurants at night, just taking it easy, sunning ourselves, and talking to friends.

A young married couple came to Side and stayed in Süleyman's father's pension. They both spoke fluent Turkish. The guy was able to understand things that were being said around the village. He asked me what the deal was with Süleyman and his wife. I explained it as I knew it. He was concerned and warned me to be careful. Also, he was very worried about my traveling alone in Turkey; he told me large numbers of young tourists had been lost and were just declared missing by the American Embassy. I assured him that I wasn't alone in Turkey and that I would be leaving soon for Cyprus anyway.

But that was just the beginning of the warnings. Later, I noticed that Süleyman's father began coming up to him at the coffeehouse and motioning him to go away with him and talk. When I asked Süleyman about this, he said, "Fucking problems again." I knew that it was about his wife, and again I was scared. But I also knew I'd be leaving the place soon. I waited every day for the money to come from my parents (even though they wouldn't have even received my letter yet). Süleyman's father came up to him a couple more times in the next few days, and Süleyman appeared increasingly concerned. I would discuss the matter with him, but nothing seemed much different than before. Through all this, I never felt fear for myself—just Süleyman. Everyone assured me that since I wasn't a Turkish citizen, I wasn't in any trouble; it was Süleyman who was in question. He could possibly go to jail for adultery. This is why we were even more careful than before not to be seen alone by anyone. We would leave the beach separately so that no village people would see us walking out of town together. Few Turks went to the beach—only young guys. And besides, we were always with other people on the beach.

Then, one afternoon, something horrible happened. I was sitting on Ali's little terrace sunning myself and I heard a woman screaming in Turkish at Süleyman, following by his angry reply. I had no time to panic. Suddenly, out of the kitchen rushed Harika. I jumped up and she screamed at me, hitting out but not touching me. Süleyman was right behind and grabbed her. Ali rushed out of the garden. Together they pushed her out of the house as she screamed foul words in Turkish.

My head was pounding and I broke out into a cold sweat. Rushing into the house, I looked out the front window, where I could peek from behind the curtain. Several neighbors had gathered around. There was general commotion. I sank down into a chair and just shook. Within maybe five minutes, someone in Harika's family led her away. Things quieted down outside. Süleyman didn't come back in. I just continued to sit there in a silent panic.

Soon Ali came back and tried to explain to me that Süleyman had gone to his father to try to find out what to do. He assured me that he'd return right away. I kept apologizing, feeling that all this commotion had been my fault, but Ali and his wife both assured me that everything was all right. All I could think of was that I wanted Süleyman to return to tell me that there really wasn't a problem. Who was I kidding?

Andrea came to see me. I talked to her about what had happened. She was bewildered, as I was. She didn't know what she'd do in that situation either.

At long last, Süleyman came back. We went to the theater separately and met there to talk. I told him I didn't think I should stay at Ali's any longer. He agreed. Why make problems for innocent people? This was the last straw for me; I wanted to leave Side very much now, but I just couldn't until the loan came. I insisted to Süleyman that I was going to leave. He broke down and cried, begging me not to go and trying to assure me that everything would work out. We had a terrible fight; I couldn't see how things were getting any better and why I should be involved in this mess anyway. But I didn't want to go to a strange Turkish village to stay by myself, and I couldn't afford to leave Turkey without more money. I longed to return to Cyprus, to a place where I felt safe and felt I could understand what was happening. I swore to myself never to go near a married man again. Actually, I never had done so in my life. If I'd known from the start that Süleyman was married, if I'd understood the situation, I never would have become involved with him.

So Süleyman looked around for a pension for me. He had trouble finding one because he wouldn't permit me to stay in several, either because he didn't approve of them or because he didn't trust their owners. Dogan had a nice pension, but Süleyman didn't like Dogan. Ali's place was "full of hippies" (the Arabs Mohammed and Arafat had returned, by the way, and said that Cap had gone to Denmark with Gry and Clemens). By nighttime, Süleyman still had not found a place. After much wandering about, he finally decided that we should sleep in one of the wooden shacks on the beach alone, way out of Side. I felt there wasn't much else I could do, figuring that any day I would be leaving anyway. So we spent an uncomfortable night in the shack.

But the next day was worse. A gendarme came and told us that Harika had complained again. He wanted us to go to the court in Manavgat and state our innocence. He assured me that there was no problem; Süleyman and I just had to say we were friends, as before. I didn't like the sound of this and couldn't understand why we had to appear at all. How many times did we have to tell them the same thing anyway?

No matter what anyone told me, I was extremely uneasy and nervous. I went to Muharrem. He didn't understand what was happening either, but he repeated that as a tourist, I didn't have to worry. Süleyman talked to his father and got the same reaction. All of the people I knew and trusted felt that this questioning was just a routine thing and that I didn't have to worry. They all told me that only Süleyman might have a problem. That eased my fears a little, but it didn't make me happy either.

So I spent a miserable day, worrying and stewing over the situation. That night, still with no place to stay, Süleyman and I walked far over the dunes and slept on the beach. I constantly had the fear that someone was following us and would see us together. But Süleyman wouldn't let me sleep on the beach alone (thank God!). He still hadn't found what he felt was a suitable pension for me. Probably I should have exerted some pressure and just found a place for myself. But again I felt the money would come any day and I'd leave.

The court appointment at Manavgat turned out to be not as bad as I'd thought. We had to sit around for ages outside waiting for them to call us. Harika and her family appeared and stared angrily at us. I felt freaky. But once the authorities had called us in, it wasn't too terrible.

We all sat at a long table. Just being in the same room with Harika and her family bothered me, but I was determined to stay calm.

Harika was questioned first, and of course, I didn't understand much. Then Süleyman was questioned.

All this probably took just a few minutes, but it seemed like ages to me. I just wanted to get out of there. Why was I involved in this anyway? I hadn't done anything wrong, I thought.

Then it was my turn. An interpreter was there for me.

"Do you know Süleyman?" he asked me.

"Yes," I replied.

"Are you friends?"

"Yes."

"Have you committed adultery with him?"

"No," I stated firmly.

After I had been questioned, Süleyman and I were instructed to report there again the next morning. I had just started to feel comfortable, but with that statement everything exploded in my mind. Why did we have to return the next morning? What was really going on?

Here is where I should have packed up and left Side. I didn't understand what was happening, and neither did anyone else I talked to. Why did Süleyman and I have to go back? The people in charge said they wanted some more questions answered. What questions? I couldn't imagine what more we could tell them.

When Süleyman and I returned to Side, again we both talked to people all day, asking questions. "What is going on? What is going to happen? Why do they continue to ask us the same questions over and over?" I was beginning to be accustomed to the horrible feeling of butterflies in my stomach and tension eating away at my insides. Through all this, I felt a great deal of fear for Süleyman, because according to everyone we talked to, he was the married one and the one breaking the law (or accused of doing so). I couldn't get into any trouble myself, they said—and they were so positive about this that I was convinced.

Süleyman and I spent another night on the beach.

CHAPTER 13

June 9, 1970

*S*üleyman and I awoke on the beach after another terrible night's sleep. It was very early in the morning and the sun was blazing down on us. As usual, we separated and went into the village, one following the other and entering by different locations. I went to the coffeehouse and waited for Süleyman, who took ages to get there. Then, just as I was thinking of how sick I was of waiting for Süleyman all the time, he arrived. We had to wait for the *dolmuş*, drinking cup after cup of çay. When the *dolmuş* finally arrived, we rode to Manavgat in silence, both of us deep in thought.

We had to wait again outside the courthouse. And unfortunately, the first people who arrived were Süleyman's wife and her whole family. I wondered what the big deal was. Why did the whole family have to be there? I just wanted to disappear.

"Little Turtle, can't we go somewhere else to wait?" I whispered.

Understanding very well why I wanted to get away, Süleyman took my arm. "Come," he replied.

He led me into the gendarme's office.

"*Merhaba,*" the gendarme greeted me, smiling and extending his hand.

"*Merhaba*. Please, please help us. I'm worried," I replied.

"No, no. It's all okay," he said. "Nothing is going to happen. Be patient. It will be over soon." Then he (the bastard, the liar [although I thought he was sweet at the time]) even sent across the street for a huge serving of *dondurma* (ice cream) for me. As I ate my treat and tried to relax, periodically the gendarme would have little conferences with Süleyman in Turkish. Then he left the room with Süleyman, leaving me alone. How I wished I could understand Turkish better. How I wished I could just walk out of there.

Finally, after what seemed to me hours, Süleyman and I were called into a large room filled with several men in suits sitting at a table. I assumed these people were lawyers. One by one they asked questions of Harika and some of her family members. Then they questioned Süleyman. As Süleyman answered their questions, I could see he was getting increasingly upset—in fact, furious! I just had to know what was going on. But how?

When the men had finished with Süleyman, it was my turn. I was called to the front of the room. An interpreter was there to translate for me.

"Do you know Süleyman?" one lawyer asked me.

"Yes," I replied.

"Do you know this man is married?"

"Yes."

"Do you know adultery is a crime in Turkey?" he continued.

"Yes," I replied, getting more and more afraid.

"Have you committed adultery with this man?"

"No, I have not," I answered, showing confidence, I hoped.

"Two witnesses have said they have seen this," the interpreter said to me.

"Who?" I asked, my fear mounting. "Where did they say it happened? When?"

The interpreter turned to a lawyer and translated my three questions. The lawyer responded. The interpreter looked at me sternly.

"You may ask this of the judge at a later time," he said.

"When?" I asked, practically begging him to help me.

"It isn't determined. Now you will go to the women's prison in Antalya."

The interpreter turned his back on me and walked away. The lawyers pushed back their chairs, picked up their papers, and one by one left the room. Not believing what I'd heard, I stared at them, my hands trembling.

What? I misheard; I didn't understand what he told me. I have to ask Süleyman. I think I'm going crazy. These thoughts ran through my head.

As I turned around to go sit down again, a man came and took me by the arm. Another man took Süleyman. We were led to another room. Getting more and more panicked, I asked Süleyman if what I had understood was correct.

"What is happening to us?" I asked him, my voice trembling with fear.

"They going to put us in jail—you Antalya, and me Manavgat." Süleyman's face was somber.

"What? That can't be true!" I screamed. "Süleyman, do something! Anything! They can't put us in jail. We haven't done anything wrong. Do something!"

My brain was swimming with panic, thoughts, and ideas. My whole body started to shake and shudder. *What in God's name am I going to do?* I thought.

In a corner of the room, an official was talking to Süleyman seriously while I watched in a state of shock and horror. Somehow, I was sure Süleyman was fixing everything. He was Turkish, wasn't he? The two of them were speaking in low voices; both of their faces were so solemn. But I was pretty sure I could count on Süleyman. At least, I sure hoped so.

Two uniformed gendarmes appeared. Suddenly, each grabbed one of Süleyman's arms and began to lead him away, leaving me there. At the same time, I saw, Süleyman's father coming up the stairs toward us. I began screaming, "Help! Come quickly!" I had never been so terrified in my life. Süleyman's father talked to them, but his and my pleas didn't help, because after a short conversation with, the gendarmes took Süleyman away. Süleyman's father followed them. Now I was left alone, completely at the mercy of the men in the room.

I sat there, shaking, and then a young gendarme approached me and took hold of my hand. He then proceeded to smear it with sticky black stuff. Suddenly, through a haze, I realized what he was doing.

"No, no," I screamed. "You can't do that. I haven't done anything wrong. I want to telephone the American Embassy. I have that right."

I may have thought I had that right; I'd been brought up to think I had certain rights. However, this situation was happening far from where I'd been brought up. And anyway, I'd never been close to such a situation in my life before.

I continued to pull my hand away from the gendarme. Then a second gendarme came to help the first. The two men tried to force my hand down on a paper for fingerprints. I resisted, but finally gave up, talking and yelling at the men in charge. All I could think of was to try to get them to call or let me call the American Embassy. I remembered I'd read many times that an American in legal trouble in a foreign country should contact the American Embassy as soon as possible. I was sure someone at the embassy would be able to help me.

But I got no answers. No one said anything to me.

Speaking Turkish now, I said, "Let me talk to the gendarme from Manavgat."

Even though that gendarme had lied to me, or at least had been wrong in his predictions, he had always treated me nicely, so I thought that maybe he could help me now. Maybe some mistake had been made.

But the answer to my request was that the gendarme from Manavgat couldn't be found.

After what seemed like a very long time, finally the authorities led me downstairs and showed me a place to wash my hands of that black junk. I waited again. At long last, an interpreter appeared, a Turkish businessman from down the road. He nicely explained to me that I had broken the Turkish law, or at least had been accused of doing so. Therefore, I would have to stay in the Antalya jail until I could be tried. He didn't know how long it would take for a trial to be arranged. I asked him if I could call the American Embassy. He said I would be able to do that from the jail. Suddenly I felt a little relief through the shock. He then brought me a plate of food. I wondered who on earth would be able to eat under those circumstances, but I somehow or other managed to eat.

After I finished my lunch, two soldiers carrying long rifles appeared. My hands were put into handcuffs. Unbelievable! One of the soldiers then asked me for enough money for bus fare for the three of us. I thought about what they would have done if I hadn't had any money. The three of us then walked to the bus station and got on the bus for Antalya, with, of course, everyone staring at me like they'd never stared at me before. I must have been in total shock by then, because the situation just didn't upset me like one would think. I had begun to feel like I was just in a weird adventure.

One soldier sat beside me and the other in front of us. During the ride, I begged the soldier beside me to just go with me to a telephone in Antalya before taking me to the jail so I could call the American Embassy. I begged and begged. He finally agreed. *Thank God,* I thought. Meanwhile, one of my thoughts during all this panic was that I was disgusted that I was missing a beautiful day. I wondered how many more I would miss—or if I'd even ever see another one.

In Antalya, we got into a taxi. Before I knew it, we'd pulled up to a building I just knew was the *hapishane (jail)*. Here were some official-looking people and some wooden benches, where I sat in a stupor, just waiting. Finally, someone came over to me and, in very simple Turkish that I could understand, told me that it was impossible to call an embassy from the jail. Then he unlocked the big steel door on the right side of the jail and let me into the women's section of the Antalya prison.

Before me were thirteen women in Turkish village dress, all standing and staring at me. And there I was, completely in shock, dressed in jeans and a T-shirt, staring back at them. Gradually, one by one, they came forward and said, "*Hoş geldiniz*" (Welcome). Welcome to the jail? A very fat woman came forward and introduced herself as *Anne* (pronounced "Ah-neh"—meaning "mother"). I was very excited because she spoke a few words of English—very few, but it was English nevertheless.

Behind me, the heavy front door was closed and the key turned in the lock. This was a sound that I learned very well and never will forget.

The narrow entryway we were in was whitewashed and filled with plants in old olive oil cans, which is typical of the Mediterranean area. There were also a couple of wooden benches there. On my left was a barred window looking into a dark room.

141

Anne took me on a tour of the *hapishane*, with the other women following behind. Turning left at the end of the entryway, I saw a courtyard. This and the entryway were open to the sky. The walls were high and whitewashed with no windows. Around the edge of the courtyard, high above us, paced a solider with a rifle. In one corner above us was a sentry box. There was also a small enclosed room off the courtyard with a tiny shower stall.

Next to the courtyard were two enclosed rooms, one with washtubs, and the toilet room (with the footprints, as usual). The other room was almost completely filled with two long wooden tables. These were the beds. Thirteen women laid out their mattresses and blankets at night and slept there in two long rows, side by side. Neither of the latter two rooms was whitewashed. The floors and walls there were both just dark, dreary concrete. The bedroom had the only window, a barred one that looked out onto the entryway. There was no way to see outside, except for the sky straight above the courtyard.

Obviously, I was in a state of shock. The enormity of what had happened hadn't set in yet. The first thing that was done was that someone sat me down. Then one of the women brought me a big plate of luscious Turkish food. I was to find out that the only food given to the inmates of the jail was bread. Each morning, a big basket of warm fresh-baked bread was brought in. *Anne* would go out every day with money from the women and buy meat, vegetables, and grains for them to cook. There were three burners to use for cooking. All the women had divided up into three groups by friendship. Anne did cooking for herself and a couple of the women in her little room off the entryway. The other two groups of women did their cooking in the courtyard. All three groups wanted to feed me and encouraged me to eat with them. It was very hard to decide what to do since I didn't want to offend anyone, yet I didn't want to eat (or shouldn't have eaten) three meals, three different times a day.

By the time I was "settled" in the *hapishane* and had eaten my lunch, it was midafternoon. I went to Anne and asked her how I could contact the American Embassy. She said she would try to call them for me the next day. The next day? I also tried to find out from her just how long I'd be in jail. "I don't know—maybe few days, maybe few months," she replied. She did speak English, but very little, maybe as much English as I did Turkish. That meant communication wasn't the greatest. I then had a brainstorm and asked her if she could call Side and ask for Helene and Muharrem; maybe they hadn't heard what had happened and they could help me.

Somehow, the afternoon, dinnertime, and evening passed. I even found myself enjoying the place in a way. All the women and I sat in the courtyard on the floor and on one bench as we talked, sang, and danced. They were full of questions for me.

"Why are you here?" one asked me.

"The police think I am guilty of committing adultery with Süleyman," I replied.

"Do you love Süleyman?" another asked.

"Yes, I do, but I'm not guilty."

"Why don't you call America and have your father come and get you out?" the fat woman with the baby asked me.

"Is your father rich?" another asked.

Believe it or not, we actually said quite a lot to each other. As a result, I found myself learning more Turkish. I was going to have to—how else could I talk to these women? They told me of another tourist who had been there a few months earlier. It seems she'd been in on a hashish charge and had stayed there three months *(God!)*. This German woman had marked off the days with chalk on the concrete walls of the bedroom. Those marks were still there.

Actually, these Turkish women were great. They didn't seem to be criminals to me. They were all very friendly and caring, and very fascinated with me. All of them were very sympathetic, yet they seemed adjusted to and happy with their surroundings. *How could they be?* I wondered. At one point during the evening, I went into the bedroom, lay on the wooden bench, and cried quietly just a little. One of the women came in and patted me, trying to comfort me. It wasn't a real cry because I felt very tense and unbelieving of the enormity of the situation. I just couldn't believe what had really happened. I was in shock. The reality hadn't yet set in.

It seemed that most of the women inmates were in jail for theft. One was in for suspicion of murder with a shovel. *Anne* called me into her room and told me I should keep my money and/or any valuables in her room because many of the women were thieves. Three of the women had their babies with them—all were boys about a year old. Before bedtime when the door to the courtyard was locked, one of the women gave me some of her bedding that I could use. Another gave me a pale pink cotton nightgown to wear. What would have happened to me if they hadn't liked me? How would I have bought food and found bedding?

The evening had been enjoyable with the conversation in the courtyard and singing and dancing. I had asked the women to sing "Rayan" and other songs that Süleyman had sung to me. They were very pleased that I liked Turkish music.

About nine at night, everyone went to bed and the door to the courtyard was locked (that *sound!*). I had been entertaining hopes of sitting out there and just thinking about the situation, but when the door was shut, I became claustrophobic. I went to my section of the wooden bed, spread out the bedding, and sandwiched myself between two other women. Lying there in the darkness, I could hear the sounds from outside the jail—horses clip-clopping by and the creaking of wagons. Occasionally a car would drive by, and sometime people's voices would reach my ears.

I lay there on that hard bed, thinking about what had happened. Prison? This was impossible. I felt like I was in the middle of a huge nightmare. Or was I going crazy?

Prison was a place one saw in the movies. One could read a book about a prison experience. In the newspapers I'd read about people who'd been imprisoned for one reason or another. In my life, I'd never known anyone who'd been arrested. I'd never even received a speeding ticket.

Up until my experience in Turkey, I'd taken my childhood and the rest of my life for granted. Now, I began to realize how lucky I'd been.

I was so very tired, though, and needed to rest. I closed my eyes and somehow, finally, fell asleep—but only for a while.

CHAPTER 14

June 10, 1970

*W*ith a start, I awoke and realized again where I was. I remembered the night before, how I'd awoken, how I'd been petrified, panicked, and claustrophobic. All the results of my mental work to calm myself during the night disappeared. The courtyard door had been unlocked in the early morning. I flew to *Anne*'s room. I must have looked like a madwoman in my long baggy pink nightgown that had been lent to me by *Anne* the day before. The guard by the door looked on with great interest as I continually yelled and screamed at *Anne*, flailing my arms around.

"Let me out of here! Please help me!" I screamed. "Please go call Helene and Muharrem in Side."

Anne was very sympathetic. She patted my shoulders and did her best to calm me down. Then, agreeing to do what she could, she left on her errand.

It wasn't long before a male warden came into our section and told me that I had visitors. Oh, the sense of anticipation and relief I felt. I was going to get out of that place, even for just a while. The warden led me upstairs. There in a large room sat Helene, Muharrem, Süleyman's father, and a stranger. I, the person who was ashamed to cry in front of anyone, burst into tears of relief. Probably they were also the tears from yesterday.

But I didn't want to cry. I wiped my eyes and tried to smile.

145

Süleyman's father had been to see a lawyer in Manavgat, and Muharrem had talked to the stranger who was sitting beside him. They told me that this man was rich and from Manavgat. Everyone there seemed sure that they could get me out of jail in a few days—maybe even the next day. I wasn't sure exactly how they planned to do it, but they seemed to think the rich man could Süleyman's father had been pull some strings. They told me not to worry, saying that Süleyman was fine and that they would be working on things for me from the outside. Helene had packed up a parcel of my things—some clothes, some English books, and some snacks and cigarettes. They also gave me some spending money, because mine was in traveler's checks that they couldn't cash. Suleyman's father was very sweet, and everyone was very encouraging. When I returned downstairs, I was completely confident in my early release—also ecstatic: a high after a tremendous low.

All the women were very interested in my possessions. Helene had even packed Süleyman's beige sweater for me, the one I had always worn on chilly days. She knew that just that item would be an emotional help. I happily told my new friends that I would be released very soon. They were glad they had been right.

The next couple of days are sort of a blur in my memory. For a while, I was fairly optimistic and tried to "enjoy" myself as much as possible. I found, however, that it was impossible to read. My mind just wouldn't let me concentrate. At one point, I went into the courtyard and attempted to lie in the sun, much to the surprise of the women. They just couldn't understand why anyone would want to be brown. The guard overhead was very intrigued by this too. Finally I gave up the idea. Actually, the heat was oppressive in that place during the day. And I wouldn't have been able to stand the sun for long without somewhere to swim and cool off. I remember welcoming the nighttime, because then the place would be more comfortable.

One day I decided I had to wash my filthy hair and take a shower. Gizem, a heavy, light-skinned woman, decided to help me. She was one of those who took special enjoyment in hovering over me, making sure I ate enough. She heated the water in a wood furnace and then proceeded to come into the little shower room with me. That really didn't please me. I didn't feel like stripping down in front of her, but I didn't know how to nicely ask her to go. So, in my modesty, I left my underwear on. I had no shampoo there. The women insisted that a bar of soap would do just fine. So Gizem proceeded to scrub me down. It was very painful. The Turks certainly believe in getting all the dirt off and out of your skin. When she was through, half my tan was gone. My hair was also in an atrocious state afterward—not only was the soap hard in it, but also I had no conditioner and could barely get a comb through it. But when we emerged from the shower room, I had many compliments from those women. "Çok güzel!" (How beautiful you look now—how clean!)

Despite our being prisoners, the mood was fairly happy in jail. There was lots of singing and dancing. The women attempted to show me how to dance. I wasn't too coordinated, but I tried.

One night, there was a big fight between two women, Fetaya and Aisha. It got pretty violent and physical. The other women tried to keep them apart. It was Anne's night off. The commotion and noise of the fight brought in the male wardens. Very roughly, they herded all of us into the bedroom area and locked us in. This was quite early in the evening. The idea of losing our courtyard privileges for the rest of the evening was horrible. Not only that, but also I was really scared because the fight was spreading—more and more people were getting into it. I huddled in a corner on the wooden bed and felt afraid and claustrophobic! Gizem came over and told me not to worry. Within an hour the problem was settled. I never could figure out exactly what had been going on. Aisha sat in a corner and cried for a long time after that.

Anne had a radio. I spent as much time as I possibly could in her room listening. She also had comfortable chairs and couch beds that were such a treat to sit on. Every so often, she'd turn on a Cyprus station and I could hear the familiar songs that I'd heard when I'd been in Nicosia. My God, why did I ever leave there? Why did I come back to such a mess?

When Thursday had gone by and I had heard nothing from anyone about my getting out of that jail, I began to get frightened again. Muharrem called Friday morning and said Helene and he couldn't come to visiting hours that day. He said Andrea would come, adding that they were still working on my case. I began to have my doubts and became nervous again. Was I ever going to get out? I realized that Mr. Karga and the rich man probably couldn't do anything for me. I'd be in jail forever. It was coming true for sure, just as I'd thought: my life was ruined!

Friday came, and along with it visiting hours. I was very glad to see Andrea. She brought little gifts for me. Our visit was like a gateway to the outside. Freedom is the most wonderful thing in the world—and I didn't have it. Andrea asked if I'd tried to contact the American Consulate, and I told her what had happened when I did try. She offered to call them for me. She was sure the Canadian Embassy helped Canadians when they are in trouble and was positive the Americans would help me. I had always thought that would be the case too, but how could I make contact with the embassy? She assured me she'd call them right away. Again, I had a small hope.

Fetaya's father visited that day also. Fetaya, one of my favorite women, was also in prison for adultery. After her father left, Fetaya sat in a corner and quietly cried. It was the first time I'd ever felt despair in one of those women. She and I had discussed our situations previously. Her lover was in the same jail as Süleyman was. Perhaps they knew each other. She had about two more years to serve of her sentence.

Fatma was an enormous, ugly woman. She and her little baby boy had their hair dyed red once a week with henna (it actually was orange). It was abominable. Fatma got into a strange mood one day and stripped down to the waist. She had enormous boobs—giant things that hung to her waist. And could she dance! Everyone got very excited and egged her on. This took place in the bedroom. Just then, a male warden came into the entryway. He got quite a sight through the barred window. Fatma just danced all the harder, her giant boobs swinging, a huge smile on her face. All the women laughed and clapped.

The women wore several layers of clothing. They all wore pajamas or bloomers, a slip over them (this is what they slept in), and over that two or three dresses and maybe a sweater. And then they wore some kind of head scarf or other head covering. Now I knew why all Turkish woman looked fat. They were very taken with my clothing though. Actually, I felt ridiculous in my Western clothes there and eventually just went around in my pink nightgown day and night. It was loose, cool, and comfortable. My jeans just were too hot. Plus, I felt almost indecent in them, not to mention my miniskirts.

Fetaya one day started going through my clothes and decided to try on a minidress. It fit her fine, but she was just too modest to take off her pajamas. Off she went, out into the courtyard to show everyone else. They all got such a kick out of that.

I spent lots of time playing solitaire. Several women were fascinated and watched me constantly. Anne then asked me to show her a card game. I tried to teach her gin, but I found the language barrier a problem in explaining the finer details. We ended up playing a very simplified and boring gin. It was even worse with the others. They must have thought American card games were for morons.

I was usually in a good mood in spite of everything. And I was eating a lot and craving exercise. After all, it was only a few steps from one part of the jail to another—and all I was doing was sitting.

So I decided to run. This was a ridiculous idea, really. The only conceivable place to run was the courtyard, which was only maybe ten meters long. I told the women I had to move, and though they didn't seem to understand what I meant, one offered to run with me. So we ran in circles around the small courtyard in the hot sun with an audience of the guards watching from above (laughing and staring) and the rest of the women (also amused and cheering us on). What a farce—especially me in that pink nightgown. The exercise didn't last long, and we never repeated it.

Food was very good in prison. I was sure I was going to put on lots of weight. The women had divided themselves into three eating and cooking groups, as previously mentioned. At mealtime, the women would have me choose which group to eat with. Then sometimes after I ate my meals, another group would bring me another plate of their food. We usually would have a big pot of stew (vegetables, sometimes a little meat) with rice and bread, and sometimes a pudding for dessert. The groups would go to the bedroom, where we'd sit on the wood beds in circles and eat. There would always be a spoon for me, even though I would have been perfectly happy to eat as they did with their bread, dipping it in the sauce and scooping up the solids. All the women in the prison had been housewives in a country where most home-cooked food is made from scratch. The three cooking groups each spent hours preparing every meal we had, so certainly the meals were really scrumptious.

One day, the women asked me if I'd contribute to the tea fund and buy the tea for the mornings. It was the least I could do. After all, I was devouring tons of their food and they had refused to let me donate money for that.

One night, all the women had quite a discussion about sex. Had I slept with Süleyman? What was he like? Did he have pubic hair—that is, did he shave it? Then one of the women wadded her dress up at her crotch in the shape of a prick and came toward me holding it, saying, "I'm Süleyman." Even though these women looked very innocent in dress and morals, they certainly talked about sex and were very interested in it. As a matter of fact, in some ways they were more sophisticated than I was; I couldn't imagine doing some of the things they did. I was too private and modest. They told numerous dirty jokes and were hysterical about them, but I couldn't always follow the Turkish.

Another thing that the women continually did was to pull the hair off their faces, since Turkish people and the Muslim religion don't like hair on the body. One would lie down with her head in the other's lap and they'd pull the hairs one by one with tweezers. They kept wanting to do this for me, but I refused.

The red-haired woman's baby usually wore only a T-shirt. The women took great delight in playing with his genitals. If this is typical among Turkish people in general, I wonder what it does to the Turkish males psychologically.

Sometime during the day on Friday, Anne came to me and said a man from the American Consulate would be visiting me during that day. My spirits soared! I dressed myself in my jeans and shirt instead of the pink nightgown. Then I waited. In the late afternoon, a representative of the US Consulate came and took my passport information. Then later on, another man came. Mr. Soykam was a Turkish lawyer from Antalya. He spoke fluent English. The American Consulate had contacted him to visit me, asking that he do what he could to help (thank God for Andrea!)

I told Mr. Soykam the entire situation as I knew it, and then he asked me quite a few more questions. When I explained what I'd been asked at the courthouse in Manavgat, he pointed out to me that I'd made two huge mistakes.

The first mistake was that I had said I knew Süleyman was married. And the second mistake I'd made was that I had said I knew that adultery is a crime in Turkey.

Telling me his fee would be $120, he offered to help me. I didn't care at that point if his fee were $1,000. I wanted out of there.

Saturday night another great thing happened. The door to the outside was opened, and this time *Anne* let everyone outside. There was a concrete wall about waist high bordering the walk to the jail and between the street and us. We stood in a mob watching the outside world for maybe ten minutes. That was such a treat! I was very happy. People, as they walked by, stared and pointed at us and looked with curiosity. I didn't care. They could look as much as they wanted. I was outside. However, this little taste of freedom was soon taken away as the guards herded us back inside. There was a male warden whom I'd seen a few times when he came into the women's side to talk to *Anne*. I begged him as we were being led back inside please to let us stay outside a little longer. All the wardens were quite amused by this, but it didn't work.

Saturday night, I awoke to hear someone getting sick. It was a terrible sound, but whoever it was, was trying to be quiet. The woman got up and lay down continually for the next hour or so and seemed miserable. Hating these things as I do, I kept holding my ears and wishing it would end.

Well, I was still in prison and wasn't sure what was going to happen. Someone was throwing up not far away. I was trying very hard to grin and bear it.

But we prisoners had been let outside for a few minutes that day. That had been very exciting. And added to that was the fact that Mr.

Soykam had come the day before and given me a tremendous amount of hope.

I slept very well that night.

CHAPTER 15

*S*unday morning, I awoke sick myself, burning with fever. I wish I had had a thermometer, because I'm sure my fever was the highest I've ever had. I was miserable. One of the women brought me my morning çay. I told her I was çok hasta (very sick). Then the dysentery started. I was very ill, thinking for a while that I'd be sick to my stomach. Fortunately, I wasn't. I was suffering enough without having to put up with that too. Weak and limping, I went to *Anne*'s room and told her also that I was "çok hasta." She gave me something—I guess it was aspirin—and told me to go back to bed.

I did what *Anne* told me to do. I had to. I had no strength or energy to move around. I flopped back down on the scratchy blanket and fell into a deep sleep.

About noon, I awoke in a sea of sweat and misery to see many faces looking down at me. The women were discussing me and appeared quite worried. *Anne* told me to get dressed, saying that they were taking me to the doctor. But I couldn't get dressed; in fact, my legs collapsed under me when I tried to get up. The women helped me put on my jeans and a T-shirt. Then *Anne* and a male warden came. Each of them put one of my arms around their neck and literally dragged me down the street, accompanied by four armed gendarmes. I couldn't walk! Never had I been so weak. As usual, it was a hot, sunny day. Lots of people were out on Sunday anyway. Everyone on the street was staring at me. I must have been quite a sight, but I didn't care.

The hospital was about a block from the jail, so it wasn't a long walk, but we weren't exactly walking. I was being pulled. Inside the hospital, several people looked at me and took a few tests. I was in such a haze that I can't remember now just what they did. One doctor said to me that I was "çok hasta." I already knew that. They told me that I was sick enough to stay in the hospital, but the hospital jail ward was already filled, so I'd have to go back to the jail. That was such terrible news. To think I'd almost made it out of the prison but barely missed because of bad luck.

I was dragged back to the *hapishane* the same way I'd been dragged to the hospital. I couldn't support my own weight. When we got to the *hapishane*, I stumbled into the bedroom, fell back onto the wooden bed, and remained there the rest of the day—and for the next few days, except for numerous trips to the concrete hole. I constantly had the symptoms of dysentery. It was all I could do to stagger there, holding onto the wall all the way. *Anne* went out and bought the recommended medicines—an obnoxious liquid that I had to take by spoon, and also pills. Of course, I had to pay for this and for the doctor's bill. For the rest of that day, I lay there sweating and thinking I probably would die.

Monday, I felt no better. I wasn't used to this. Usually when I'd been ill, I would start feeling better before too long. This time, I didn't.

In the late afternoon, Mr. Soykam came back as promised. I had to be helped out to the entryway to talk to him. I greeted him in my pink nightgown. He was quite concerned with the change in me. I must have looked like hell. But he had good news. He'd visited Side and found that Süleyman's wife was willing to drop the charges, but her brother was the strong one who had a grudge against Süleyman. After he'd attacked Süleyman with a knife and been put in jail, he was now determined to put Süleyman in jail. It was clearly an act of revenge on the part of the brother. No one seemed to care that much about Süleyman's and my "fooling around." So Mr. Soykam had gone into Manavgat that morning and talked to the prosecutor. He said he'd gotten a guarantee that we both would be released on bail if I'd leave the country, or at least the Side area.

Mr. Soykam had gotten Ian, Muharrem, and Halil to act as my witnesses. The trial had been set for Friday morning (this was Sunday). Mr. Soykam practically promised me I'd be released after that. He assured me he'd had to work very hard to get such an early trial date. Otherwise, I'd have had to wait for months. I believe that.

Back to bed I went, feeling mentally better but physically just as bad. The women kept trying to get me to eat, but I just couldn't stand the sight of food. This really concerned them; I hadn't eaten for two days. Monday was another very sick day for me. I wasn't getting any better.

Tuesday was visiting day. Süleyman's friend Mehmet visited me. That really made me happy. Also Helene and Muharrem were there, and Andrea too. All were very concerned about my sickness because I just wasn't improving. But at least I had felt well enough to make it to the barred window to talk to them. Süleyman's friend bought me an English magazine. I was very impressed. Helene and Muharrem had visited Süleyman in his jail and said he was fine, telling me he sent his love. Yes, they had shaved his head. Thinking of Süleyman without his beautiful hair made me feel worse.

Now I was counting the days until Friday. The time just dragged by. Because I felt so miserable, I lay most of the time in bed. I still had dysentery, but I hadn't eaten anything to encourage it, so I was losing weight fast. I had no strength to move. Once I drank a glass of *çay*, which just tasted terrible.

Thursday, I did feel a little better, which was a good thing, because I had to get dressed. Anne hired a horse-and-carriage taxi and took me to the courthouse for fingerprinting and to have some forms filled out. In one office, I felt so bad that I tried to sit down. The man in charge yelled at me for that. *Anne* said later that he'd been upset that I was showing disrespect. But it wasn't that. It was just that I couldn't stand up. However, even though I felt terrible, I mentally felt fantastic because I was out of that jail. I also had high hopes of getting out the next day for good. But I was afraid to be too optimistic. After all, people had told me many wrong things before.

After the fingerprinting, the officials told me to go outside the building and wash my hands at a little fountain in the garden. No one came with me. I felt free at last. I wanted that moment never to end.

I could see the sea from there. Everything looked so gorgeous that I promised myself that I would never forget the feeling of freedom, of being able to walk down the street free, go where I wanted.

On the way back to the jail, I saw a watermelon stand. Finally feeling hungry and thirsty, I wanted some melon. *Anne* stopped the carriage and bought some for me. This was very exciting. She told me that eating something cold would be bad for me, but I knew I needed liquids and only cold things had any appeal. As soon as we got back to the jail, I cut open the melon, ate a few bites, and offered some to my friends. Naturally, after all those days of not eating, I couldn't eat much.

The following was written from prison. I wanted to keep in touch with my family so they wouldn't worry when they didn't hear from me. But at the same time I didn't want them to know the truth, to know that I was in prison. They'd go crazy. I tried to cover up what was going on, which made this a very difficult letter to write. In fact, what I let them know was that I was very sick, which in itself would have worried them a great deal. Also, in the prison, I'd convinced myself that only love could have possibly gotten me into that situation, so I told my parents that now it was the real thing.

June 17, 1970

Dear Family,

I know it's been a while since I've written, but it's been literally impossible. I've been flat on my back with some vile disease (I would guess it's dysentery or bad intestinal flu or something). I have been to the hospital in Antalya and have had to spend a small fortune on medicine and shots. I received your letter saying you thought I was penniless, and I kind of laughed then, but it's not funny now. I am penniless and living off borrowed money of Helene and Muharrem. Friends here always help in a crisis.

I asked before for a loan of money until August 1, and I realize it's too soon for it to have arrived even if you acted immediately. Mail is so slow. But now, as I'm sure you see, I'm in desperate need. I have to leave Turkey as soon as possible and begin working in Cyprus. I detest financial worry. I know my problem now is my own fault and I should suffer for it. Yet I can't work in Turkey, and I can't get out of Turkey to work without money. God!

I want to write more, but I'm so sick and weak, I can't. But I didn't want you to worry because I hadn't written. This sickness will pass soon—it's improved already. And now I'm so skinny.

I think I asked for $300. If you do send more (not necessary), please make one bank draft for $300 and put the rest in a separate draft. Turkish liras

156

aren't considered good money, and you lose money when you try to convert them. I would cash the rest in Cyprus.

It's quite likely that Helene will go to Cyprus with me or come soon after. Both of us—and Andrea too, for that matter—are really in love with our Turkish village boyfriends. If it isn't love with me, then it's something much different and more beautiful than I've experienced. At any rate, it's possible that Muharrem and Süleyman can dig up the money to get to Cyprus. If so, we'll all see what happens in a culture I would place far, far below the United States in development.

Turkey is a rotten hellhole. Any wish for achievement is stifled for anyone without lots of money. Süleyman and Muharrem both didn't have much schooling because the advanced schools were miles away and there was no transportation. Also they both had big families. When they work, they make three hundred lira (thirty dollars) a month for a twelve to fifteen hours a day. I wouldn't work either (they work seven days a week). I detest Turkey for keeping its people down. I've been reading the current *Time magazine lately, and no matter how bad the United States seems now, thank God, you're Americans. I mean it. Believe me, I'm learning from the other side.*

I'll elaborate more in a few days when I feel better. There's a lot more I have to tell.

Thank you for any help you can give. I'm ashamed to be this age and having to ask you for help. Believe me, I really am.

I love all of you, and I miss you terribly. Please write soon.

Love,
Karen

CHAPTER 16

June 18, 1970

Friday morning, I awoke early and dressed in my best jeans (which now were way too big and kept falling down my hips) and my rubber flip-flops with one broken strap. My hair was atrocious and hadn't been washed since Gizem had washed it with soap over a week prior. Of course, I had barely combed it during my illness. I tried to do something with it and finally ended up braiding it down my back. My tan had faded and I looked a sickly white. The scrubbing in the shower hadn't helped that either—what tan remained was patchy. I had a tube of lipstick and some mascara with me. Using those, I tried to make myself look human, but it sure didn't work. Not only that, but also I was still was running quite a high fever and barely had any strength. However, my hopes for that day kept me going.

I sat in the entryway and waited for Mr. Soykam. It seemed like he'd never come, as he was late. But finally he appeared, much to my relief. He had hired a taxi and said he wasn't allowed to drive me in his private car. I had to pay the taxi fare, which he added to his fee. A soldier with the inevitable rifle came along. During the ride, Mr. Soykam lectured me about my future.

"I'm shocked at the fact that you have a bachelor's degree from a university, that your father is a university professor, and that here you are," he said, regarding me sternly. "What are you doing?

"Do you really want Süleyman?" he continued. "He is a nothing, will never become anything. If you really want a Turk, why don't you go to Istanbul and find an educated one? I've seen your passport picture. I can't believe you now look so terrible, when once you were so beautiful!"

He went on scolding me and told me he felt I should get out of Turkey and out of this situation immediately. He made me promise not to see Süleyman after the release—not only for my own legal safety, but also for my own personal sake.

I listened to him and agreed with every word he said.

When we arrived in Manavgat, we went to the courthouse. Many other people and we were seated on benches in the hall, just waiting. I saw my friends from Side and also noticed Harika's family standing there. I felt very weak and in a daze. And no matter what Mr. Soykam had predicted, I was still afraid that he wouldn't be able to get me released from prison.

Then two soldiers came in leading Süleyman in handcuffs. This was one of the most shocking sights of my life. He hardly looked like himself; his head was shaven, his eyes looked enormous, and of course his wrists were held together with those atrocious handcuffs. Tears started rolling down my cheeks. Then I looked over and saw Süleyman looking at me. His eyes were very sad; he was full of emotion. It was an awful moment for both of us.

We were the first case. All the concerned people were led into the courtroom. This room looked very similar to US courtrooms, but rustic and very simple. I sat on a bench with Mr. Soykam. The lawyers questioned my Turkish witnesses and had interpreters for the Canadians. All my witnesses said they had seen no evidence of adultery. Each one stated that Süleyman and I were just friends.

Then they questioned Harika and her family. Details are fuzzy now, and since I couldn't follow all the Turkish, I'm not sure exactly what was said. I do know that the witnesses couldn't cite any actual cases of adultery. Nobody had seen us making love. No one had proof that we'd stayed together overnight.

Next, the lawyers talked to Süleyman. I didn't understand a word of it. Then I was next. For this, I had to stand in front of the judge. Being as weak as I was, I constantly had to keep grabbing onto a bench!

Mr. Soykam mentioned to the judge that I'd been very sick, but that had to be obvious to anyone who saw me.

Mr. Soykam had told me that the main point he wanted me to stress was that I hadn't known Süleyman was married when I met him and that I had not committed adultery with him ever. When the two of us discussed what I was going to say previously, I realized that I hadn't made a mistake at the courthouse the day we were imprisoned. The lawyer had asked his question differently: "Do you know Süleyman is married?" I had answered, "Yes." However, this time the question was "Did you know Süleyman was married when you began your friendship with him?" The truth, and my answer, was "No. I didn't."

In Turkey, actual visual evidence for adultery has to be shown before the accused is judged guilty. It is true that no one had actually seen Süleyman and I having sex and that none of the accusers had proof that we had slept together, but we certainly had been in enough situations that would seem adulterous (like going to Istanbul together). Of course, when I was asked if I'd been adulterous, I said no.

Then the judge announced that we would be released from prison as of that day and that we would each have to pay $200 bail, which would be returned after the trial, if we were found innocent. The trial was set for mid-July. Mr. Soykam said I wouldn't have to appear since I wouldn't be in Turkey. Harika broke down in angry tears.

After this, Mr. Soykam led me into another, small room and asked me if I had the money for my bail. Luckily for me, my mother's money order had just arrived in Side and Helene had brought it along. The money would just cover that and the lawyer's fees. Later, Muharrem talked to me quietly and said he wanted to arrange a meeting place for Süleyman and me that night. He told me to go to the waterfront in Antalya to a specific place and wait there at seven. I listened to him and agreed, but figured I probably wouldn't and certainly shouldn't, as I was very afraid.

Even Tarik's father showed up at the trial and congratulated me on getting out of prison. Soon Mr. Soykam and I left for Antalya, taking the money order to the bank to cash it. Then we visited some office buildings in Antalya and did some paperwork for my release. Finally, he took me back to the jail (horrors!) to get my things, saying he'd return in an hour with the release papers. I couldn't bear the thought of being in that place again, but what could I do? I gathered up my stuff and told the women what had happened. All of them were genuinely pleased for me despite the fact that I was getting out and they were staying there. I sat in the entryway on a bench because I couldn't bear to wait farther inside for Mr. Soykam. During that time, the authorities brought in a sixteen-year-old Turkish girl who had just been arrested for adultery. She was very pretty and young. I couldn't believe that this "child" was being imprisoned. But then there is a lot I can't believe about that country, even now.

At long last, Mr. Soykam came. I hugged all the women and *Anne* goodbye. I felt a genuine sadness about leaving them, but not about leaving the *hapishane*. Freedom—what a release!

CHAPTER 17

We drove to Mr. Soykam's office, where he called the American Consulate in Izmir to see if they'd cover my bail expenses. No, that was impossible, they said (as I'd thought). Mr. Soykam was very indignant about that and didn't see why the Americans wouldn't support their own people. I had to pay for that phone call and also the numerous tips that he kept giving everyone. It seemed he was very free with my money, yet I was now out of prison and the money just didn't seem to matter that much anymore. The freedom meant more than the money.

Mr. Soykam then took me to a hotel on a main street in Antalya and found a room for me. I had told him to find a cheap one. Indeed, the one he found was reasonable. Then I went upstairs and finally was alone. How good that felt! Helene and Muharrem had promised to meet me the next day.

After sitting inside and recuperating for a while, I finally decided that I should really wash my hair and take a good shower. This I did. It felt wonderful just to be by myself. And get clean again. I didn't feel like eating yet, so I didn't eat.

I was trying to keep busy, to keep my thoughts on having been released from the prison. I didn't want to think about the fact that Muharrem had set up a rendezvous for Süleyman and me. I felt like I was being pulled in two directions. First, it seemed preposterous to me that I'd even consider for one minute going to meet Süleyman. Who knew what would happen if I did? And what would be the consequences if we were seen? What if Harika or someone in her family were there?

Why was my mind wandering to him, wishing I could see him, wanting to be with him? Was I crazy?

Secondly, I kept trying to convince myself that no one could see us, thinking that if someone did, we'd be sitting on a bench by the sea, which is not illegal. My reasoning told me that it was ridiculous to think meeting him was dangerous. Why was it?

I couldn't sit still. I couldn't rest. I debated long and hard about whether or not to meet Süleyman. It was that small possibility of danger that terrified me.

Finally, I decided to be brave or stupid—however you want to look at it—and go sit by the sea anyway and just wait to see what would happen. No matter what I told myself, I loved Süleyman in my way. And I had missed him while I was in jail. I wanted to be with him. It was definitely a huge risk, but I went.

When I got to the meeting place, Süleyman was already waiting for me. It felt very strange to be with him again. We sat and talked and compared our experiences. He'd had it much worse in jail than I had. He told me that not only had his head been shaven, but also his pubic area. And then the jail was very crowded; twenty-five men were stuffed and crammed into a room big enough for ten. Two or three had to share the same bunk. Lots of hash had been smuggled and everyone was stoned all the time. However, a couple of times, the wardens had let Süleyman out to swim in a little pond behind the jail. That had been his only pleasure.

I told him that if I'd been there, I would have gone insane with claustrophobia.

Looking back on it now, I know I was crazy to even see Süleyman, since I'd just been safely released from the jail. To take a chance of being caught and put back in was short of completely insane. But I had convinced myself in the jail that I must love Süleyman or else I never would have gotten into that predicament in the first place. I had to somehow justify my actions, even though deep down I knew it wasn't true and that the situation was just as Mr. Soykam had said: "impossible." Still, it seemed very good to see Süleyman again and to

163

share what had happened to each of us. We walked through the park by the sea and talked and talked.

Finally, we returned to my hotel. Süleyman had decided that he would stay in the same hotel as I—and I'm sure he expected to stay in my room. However, for "safety's sake," he went in alone and registered for a private room. Soon after, I came in and went upstairs. Süleyman was sitting in the hall outside my room. We both noticed that the clerk was hanging around and staring at us. He disappeared for a few minutes. Finally Süleyman came over to me and began talking. At that moment, the clerk appeared and told Süleyman that he couldn't stay in the hotel after all. We found out later that Mr. Soykam had warned the hotel staff about Süleyman coming and told them not to let him talk to me.

This, given my typical rebellion against authority—even after all that had happened—made me furious. Telling the clerk that I wouldn't stay there either, I picked up my few things and left with Süleyman.

That was crazy and I knew it, but craziness seemed to be compelling me. Fortunately, Süleyman knew about a tiny pension off the main streets of Antalya. We went there and got a room together. I truly feel that Harika's brother was a fool not to have tailed Süleyman after our release. What evidence he would have found. Still, I think the intelligence level was pretty low in that family. Mr. Soykam had confirmed that.

That night was the most comfortable one I'd spent in ages, even though I had begun getting sicker. This time my tonsils were bothering me (I knew about tonsillitis from previous experience). Süleyman and I discussed what to do. He said—and I agreed—that he could no longer stay in Antalya. Helene had decided to go to Cyprus with me. It was going to take her a few days to get ready to go. Besides, we had to wait a few days for the boat that sailed from Alanya. So Süleyman decided to go back to Side and come to visit me in Antalya periodically.

The next day, I was sicker yet, but we managed to get me down to the waterfront to meet Helene and Muharrem. It was extremely hot that day. I had no strength at all. The four of us tried to walk around the park area, but I kept having to sit down—anywhere—to get my strength back. Helene bought some fruit and tried to force me to eat, but it was simply no use. Helene and I did make plans to meet in Alanya a few days from then so we could catch the ship to Cyprus.

Süleyman helped me find another hotel, a quite nice one on a lighted street. First, he took me to a restaurant that had an outside section. As we looked over the choices of food to eat in the kitchen, my stomach started turning over. I begged him to take me back to the hotel, insisting that I didn't want to eat.

"But you sick and you must eat!"

"Little Turtle, please believe me. I can't eat, and it's because I'm sick. If we don't leave here now, I'll throw up!"

This finally convinced him. We went quickly back to the hotel.

However, now he was in a temper. I tried to explain to him that when someone is really sick, one doesn't feel like eating much. We argued and argued. Just like the women in the jail, Süleyman—I guess like all Turks—had a different conception of what one should and shouldn't do when one is sick. At last, I agreed that if he went out and bought "something" for me to eat, I'd try to eat it.

So he went out. And back he came with a tray loaded with food. I tried and tried to pick at the food, feeling worse every minute. When he had to leave to catch the bus back to Manavgat, he made me promise that I'd eat every bite. Ha! I couldn't eat it, leaving the tray for the hotel clerk to pick up. The next day, the clerk told Süleyman that I'd left the food untouched. He argued with me all over again.

I slept in a sweat through the night and awoke in the morning knowing for sure now that I had tonsillitis. I could hardly swallow. Süleyman came up for part of the afternoon. I told him I wanted to go to the beach. No matter how sick I was, I just had to get in the water again, cool off, and get some color back into my skin. So we caught a bus to the Antalya beach several kilometers out of town. The water in Antalya is gorgeous, turquoise, and perfectly clear, but the beach is rocky. Even though I felt pretty bad, I did enjoy myself—and the water felt wonderful. While waiting for the bus back to Antalya, though, I started feeling worse and very queasy. I kept wanting to sit down. Süleyman couldn't understand that either. I thought I would collapse.

When we got back to the hotel, I had Süleyman go out and get me some penicillin at the drugstore (thank God for not having to have prescriptions in that country). After getting my penicillin, Süleyman explained that he thought he should be around Side that night for appearances' sake. I agreed. He promised to call me and to show up the next day. We would be leaving for Alanya Monday. He thought maybe he'd dare to stay over in Antalya Sunday night.

Sunday, feeling much better, I decided to lie in the sun on the roof while waiting for Süleyman. He called about noon and said he'd be there in the late afternoon. On the way back to my room, I saw three Turks who tried to talk to me. They were college students from Ankara and quite good-looking. They didn't speak any English, but we managed to get some ideas across to each other. Later, they saw me heading up to the roof (dressed in my bikini, but wearing clothing over it). About half an hour later, I, lying in the sun with my eyes closed, was suddenly surprised when one of these men flopped down on top of me. It scared me to death. "*Git, git, pis köpek*" (Go, go, dirty dog) I screamed at him. Almost instantly, he apologized, backed off, and left. I was sick of this country and all the bastards in it. For the rest of the afternoon, I stayed on the roof and thought about how much I hated Turkey.

When Süleyman arrived, I told him about what had happened on the roof. I knew I shouldn't have told him because of his furious jealousy and temper, but still I felt I wanted to. After his first rage, ("I going to kill him"), I made him promise not to harm the man. But still, he went downstairs and told the manager of the hotel, who later talked to the man who'd done it. After that, the college guys stayed well away from us, eyeing us from a distance.

We went for a walk in Antalya and ran into Mehmet (the one who'd visited me in the jail). I was still dragging along and quite weak, but the tonsillitis was clearing up. That night, we watched an outdoor American cowboy movie from the hall window in the hotel. Mehmet visited us for a while too.

My feelings about Süleyman were confused at this time. I knew I was leaving, and I was glad about it. I couldn't wait to get away from that country. Physically, Süleyman still turned me off in some ways. He persisted in being rough with me. I just couldn't take that anymore. He looked terrible with his shaven head. Any romantic future, even short range now, was so obviously impossible that the whole thing seemed ridiculous to me. He kept talking about going to Cyprus with

Muharrem when they could get passports and money. Emotionally, there still was obviously some feeling there, but it was fading. I felt relief that I was leaving soon.

June 23, 1970

Tuesday morning we awoke early, packed my things, and caught the bus for Alanya. I was very nervous as we approached the road to Side, then Manavgat, and felt such relief as we passed on and headed for Alanya. No one from Side was going to be in Alanya, I was pretty sure, but you never knew about Antalya, because a lot of people from Side shopped there.

At the bus stop in Alanya, we caught a horse-drawn taxi. The driver took us to a hotel on the outskirts of town. The rooms were cheap and nice. Süleyman called the bus station to see if Helene and Muharrem had arrived there yet from Manavgat, but they hadn't. He left a message for them to call the hotel, which they did about an hour later. They took a room in the same hotel.

I was feeling a lot better now—in fact, I even ate a very light lunch in the hotel, much to Süleyman's happiness. Then we went down to the castle area and bought the boat tickets to Cyprus for the next morning—at five o'clock. Helene and Muharrem explored the castle, and Süleyman and I went to the beach. So much of the fun and gaiety had left our relationship. It was now either both tense and strained or highly emotional.

That night was sad and depressing. Helene and Muharrem, so much in love, were miserable, whereas my good feelings for Süleyman were beginning to return. Again, I felt I loved him. I seemed to be on an emotional seesaw. Of course, we made all kinds of plans about how we'd meet again, how Helene and I would get jobs, how the guys would get to Cyprus, and how we'd live happily ever after. I felt especially bad for Helene's current predicament, because I knew she and Muharrem had something especially good between them.

June 24, 1970

Wednesday morning, we left the hotel in the dark and walked to the dock. The boat was waiting there. Helene bought some food for the trip. After a short wait, Helene and I boarded the boat and stood there talking to the two guys who were standing on the dock. Finally, the boat pulled slowly away and headed out to sea. It was amazing how long we could see the two of them on the dock waving, tall, handsome Muharrem and short, bald-headed Süleyman. When they were like two ants, they walked off the dock. And the mountains of Turkey and the village of Alanya grew smaller and smaller until only the horizon was left.

CHAPTER 18

Our ferryboat ride from Turkey to Cyprus should have been a gorgeous trip. Under normal circumstances, it would have been. But Helene and I were in anything but normal circumstances. She was absolutely miserable, crying with sadness sometimes sand throwing up over the railing of the boat other times. She was terribly seasick and heartsick.

On the other hand, I was having mood swings. First, I was euphoric, happy that I was free and that I was going to another country to try a new life. Then I would fall into the depths of misery, missing Süleyman already and still in shock at having been in prison for ten days. Sometimes I would look around me, at the clear turquoise water of the Mediterranean and the blue sky above me, and tell myself, *Enjoy this. After all, it's not every day you'll be on such a perfect boat trip.*

But my happiness was very short-lived, as I dissolved into tears every time I thought about Süleyman and his sweet smile.

Finally, I took a pad of yellow lined paper and a pen and wrote a long-overdue letter to my family. After all, I'd been writing half-truths to them ever since I'd left the States. And I'd written that letter from jail, not even telling them where I really was. It was time I told them everything.

June 24, 1970
Nicosia, Cyprus

Dear Family,

Thank you for sending the money. It arrived quickly. Thank you.

This is going 0to be a difficult letter to write. Right now I'm on a ferryboat to Cyprus with Helene. I'm going to tell you about an event that happened recently. What follows is something that happened to me recently and that I think would be unfair to keep from you. I considered for a long time not telling you, but it's a part of my life that has affected me greatly, so I feel you deserve to know. However, I waited until all danger had passed. I am now safely out of Turkey and intend never to go back.

A couple of days after I wrote you about the money, the gendarme commandant of Manavgat asked Süleyman and me to go the following Monday to Manavgat. He said Süleyman's wife had complained about us. He said we'd have to answer a few questions and that it was nothing to worry about.. Nevertheless, not liking the sound of it, I became concerned.

On Monday we went there and were asked to give a statement about our relationship. We both said we were good friends, that Süleyman was learning English from me and that we were not sexually involved.. Then Süleyman's wife, Harika, came in and claimed she knew we had committed adultery. We were all told to come back the next day.

Süleyman and I went back to Side and talked to people. We knew for a fact that no one had ever seen us committing adultery. We also knew that adultery is a crime in Turkey. Side is a small village. Süleyman and I had been very discreet. We had been very careful because of village gossip and also danger. He and his wife lived together about six months out of the four years they were married. Anyway, in the opinion of everyone who knew anything about Turkish law, we had no problems. We had sound alibis for almost all times, and we were almost always with people or in a public restaurant.

Tuesday we went to Manavgat again. Süleyman and I were taken to various rooms, where we sat and waited and worried. Finally, we went into an office where one man typed and one man asked questions (I had an interpreter). An attorney talked to Süleyman first. I watched him closely. Toward the end of the questioning, I saw his arms stiffen slightly and his eyes change. No one else could tell, but I know him very well and I knew something horrible was happening.

Then the attorney talked to me. He asked me if I knew Süleyman, if I knew he was married and that adultery was a crime in Turkey. I said yes to those questions. They asked me if I had committed adultery. I said no.

After that, the attorney told us we were going to jail.

My immediate reaction was a stunned anger. I started protesting. The attorney told us to go upstairs. Then I did explode. I said, "Call the American Embassy," and tried getting Süleyman to ask why we hadn't been given a chance to defend ourselves. They started pulling Süleyman out of the room. His father was there, and Suleyman said, "My father will help us." Then they took him away with two gendarmes to the prison in Manavgat. Meanwhile, other people were trying to fingerprint me. I was fighting them, saying "Why?" in Turkish. God, I wished then I'd really learned Turkish well. I told them in Turkish they had to get me someone who spoke English immediately (and they did). I was furious with anger, undoubtedly in shock, and I felt the whole thing was absurd The English schoolteacher they brought in as an interpreter explained that there was no proof that we had committed adultery. The "witnesses" just suspected it. He said I could call the embassy from the prison. I still did not understand why I was going to prison without a trial. He said they would set the trial date later, but sooner because I'm a foreigner. I calmed down a little, gave my fingerprints, and went with the two soldiers on the public bus to Antalya. What a disgrace. Even worse, I had to pay transportation for all three and their way back (what a really chintzy government).

In the prison, I said again I wanted to call the American Embassy. I was told, "There's no telephone here," and put me in the women's section of the jail. How do I describe how I felt? Twelve Turkish women, three with babies, staring at me. A fat guardian who speaks a little English. I think I still must have been in shock, because I wasn't really that upset. I ate lunch and tried talking to the women there. I asked Anne (her name is Turkish for "mother"), the guardian, to please telegraph Helene and Muharrem in Side. She said I wasn't allowed to telephone the American Embassy.

Somehow I got through that night. It was hell. I became extremely claustrophobic and truly panicked. The next morning I was still really bad—and thank God, Helene and Muharrem and Süleyman's father came before the telegraph had been sent. What relief. They came with a rich man, so I was allowed to see them (otherwise I would have had to wait three days until visiting day). They said they'd write a petition and that I should probably be released in two or three days. And they brought me food, books, clothes. I felt great relief and thought I could make it.

Friday came—Andrea, Helene, and Muharrem came to visit. Andrea said, "You must telegraph the American Embassy." I said I'd tried but couldn't. She said she would. That afternoon, a representative came from the consulate and took my passport information. He said a lawyer would come the next day (there had been no answer to H and M's petition).

171

Saturday a lawyer came, said the fee was $120 (he spoke good English). I told him the problem, and he said he'd get me out as soon as possible. He took all my remaining money ($60) as a "deposit." Sunday he said he'd go to Side and investigate.

Sunday I woke up with a high fever and dysentery. By now, I was so sick that the guardian and men's guardian and four gendarmes literally dragged me to a nearby hospital. They wanted me to be hospitalized, but there wasn't a room for a female prisoner (because men were using it). So I went back full of shots and with three different prescriptions. I was really sick.

Monday—still miserably sick. Lawyer, Helene, and Muharrem, and a good friend of Süleyman's from Antalya all came to visit. Lawyer said, "Good news." He'd talked the judge into the fastest trial ever (Friday) and had a promise that Süleyman and I would go free on Friday. The people had no case. No one had witnessed adultery.

Somehow I lived through the next few days, but I was horribly sick and weak, and other people in the jail were getting sick. I was also a psychological wreck. I wrote you from the jail but couldn't tell you everything then. My money went to the lawyer.

Friday we went to Manavgat. I thought I would die when I saw Süleyman come down the hall. They shave men's heads in Turkish jails, and he was in handcuffs. Like a murderer! All his gorgeous hair was gone. How humiliating. I understood little of my own trial except what the English-speaking witnesses said. I was so sick that I could hardly stand there. And my pants were falling off because I'd lost so much weight. At the end, the judge said we had to pay 2,500 lira ($250) apiece as bail. Eventually (months, I think) this will be returned. Süleyman's father paid his, and your letter had just come. There was nothing I could do but use my Cyprus money to pay that bail. We cashed the check, paid $250 of it to Manavgat and $60 to the lawyer. And since we get 12 lira to the dollar (tourist rate), I actually got about $360 in lira from the check. I was left with about $50 worth of lira, which brought me to Cyprus. I now am almost broke again. But Helene and I will be staying at a friend's and we hope to work soon. I'll make it somehow. And I hope that $250 is returned by my lawyer quickly. I've written Dick telling him to send the August money to you. Would it be possible for you to get the remainder (I think $543) here by August for me? Then I'd have it faster than having to wait for Dick to get it here. I'm going to be really scrimping.

Please don't hate Süleyman for what happened. The whole thing was the result of an insane country with asinine laws. And to say the least, some of their citizens are extraordinarily out of their minds. I hate Turkey's laws and I'll not return there. Those ten days were absolute hell. At some points, I wanted to die—and I've never felt that *before. Turkish prisons are horrible. The food given to the prisoners is bread and water. You eat what people bring, or you have the guardian buy something for you and then you cook the food yourself. The women there were positively beautiful to me: fed me, washed my clothes, talked in simple Turkish for me. One gave me a place on the bed (a long wooden table—you have to bring your own mattress and bedding, and of course I didn't have any). I want to forget it. I've recovered. It's all like a nightmare now.

I saw Süleyman after prison in Antalya and then he took me to Alanya to get the boat. I still love him but also realize that this may not be an "everlasting" love. The jail did not change either of us. He plans to come to Cyprus in a month or so when he gets up the money, and Muharrem is coming to be with Helene. (Turks are charged a lot for their passports, and taxes are $100—and then he will have to buy a large sum of dollars at a high rate of exchange.)

I'll write more soon. I hope I'll never have to write such a horror story letter to you again.

Love,
Karen

Helene and I landed in Cyprus and quickly made new lives for ourselves. She went to Kyrenia (in the Turkish sector of the island on the north coast) and worked in a hotel as a waitress. I stayed in the Capital, Nicosia, and found a job as a barmaid in a discotheque, Skorpios. With that job, I was given free lodging in a room above the disco.

I was lucky that Skorpios was frequented by upper-class Cypriots and foreigners, as I was treated well and enjoyed my new job. I even started dating a Cypriot, a Brit, and a man from the UN Peacekeeping Force. The dating was all casual and platonic. I'd learned not to get too involved too quickly.

Following are the first three letters that I received from Süleyman. These letters show what was happening to our relationship from Süleyman's point of view. I haven't changed a word of these letters. Süleyman couldn't write English, so he dictated to people who at least could write a bit. Some of these people wrote what he said word for word; others tried to correct his English. But Süleyman's meaning was clear.

Finally, I have copied my attorney's letters to me. Mr. Soykam had a pretty good command of the English language, but sometimes his way of expressing himself was unusual, to say the least. Mr. Soykam's letters tell about the progress of the trials.

I have included all these letters because they are a part of this whole story.

Receiving these letters from Turkey affected me a great deal. I had felt I'd escaped Turkey and the dangers there. However, when I did manage to escape, I had trouble forgetting the wonderful things I'd experienced.

I had become used to the simplicity of life in Side. I had forgotten many habits I'd been used to all my life. While in Side, I didn't care if I wore the same outfit every day until it was dirty, only then changing to a second one. This was natural, I felt, and I resented having to think of a different outfit to wear each day in Cyprus. I'd lost any longing for material things. I didn't need a car in Side. I could walk anywhere, and there were minibuses to take me to nearby towns.

But, of course, I'd left behind a lover. That passion hadn't stopped once I left him behind. I could live in Cyprus and try to forget, but when letters from Süleyman arrived, I'd read them and cry. I missed him very much, but I also knew logically that I'd never see him again.

That was not easy for me.

***

This letter was dictated by Süleyman to Muharrem on June 25, 1970.

My Dear Karen,

First I have to sey this is my writting but Süleyman words. Hallo dear. I am letele tertel. We came from Alanya. After I am writting to you. I want too tell you reely dear after one our you left from mi my haert was not in same plase it was working out of my body. I love you like a krayse!! if you can andreste mi. first nite in side with out you. side was dark for mi. I couldn't sleep. What can I du I shut make my haert as a raks for few weeks. I know we will fine each other in short time and we will forget evry think from the past. and we will be happy in that time.

Darling. you know this allse. I have no one on the world exsept you. I am waiting evry dey letter from you. pealese writt me. Soon your Süleyman or letel tertl.

I love you! XXXXXXXXXXX
Süleyman

***

This letter was dictated to Andrea by Süleyman.

Dear Karen,

I am so happy. After such a long time at last the first letter from you. I was waiting every day at the Postane and never anything. Every day it was worse and worse. I miss you so much and I'm in such a hurry to see you again. I was so worried about you until I got the letter but now I know you are all right it is better but I am still alone. Every day I think I want to go to the beach but I can't go without you. Every night I want to go to the Diskotek but not if you are not here. It is so hot here in the day but at night it is too cold because you are so far away and I think about you all the time, *benim bebek [my baby]*.

I don't want to stay in Turkey anymore, I only want to be where you are, with you all the time. I love you so much, and it is such a long time since I have seen you. Even if I can come to Cyprus tomorrow it is too long time. I am happy you have a job in the Diskotek because I know you can send me money to be with you sooner.

I am sending you million times million kisses. I miss you so much. I don't know what to do without you because there is nothing here. You are everything for me and you are so far away. Hurry and work so I can come soon.

*

Süleyman
XX love Andrea and Sweet Tarik

***

This letter was dictated by Süleyman to Muharrem.

Darling my Tertl,

I got al your letters in two deys. I was happy. You think I am not thinking about you, but believe me evry minute I am thinking about us, *sevgilim [darling]*.

I stard to get my pasport. it is not going to takae long tim to have it. Just fwe deys I'm raely shure in three deys I will have it so I am wateing money and nwes from you. if it's posabl send me much money maby I will have trubl in the border so they ask from mi a adress from Cyprus. I geave your adrese—Amerika express that will be o.k. So Karen Muharrem hello from

175

me to you. Happy deys. How is Helene I hoop she didnot chanch her mind she still love me. give my mind with this words to my darling. I hav ruit yesterde and I writ tonigth to her.

Thank you, xxx Muharrem
Süleyman XXXXXXXXXXXX

***

The following is my lawyer's first letter to me.

Ethem Soykam
Avukat (lawyer)
Antalya

18 July 1970

Dear Karen,

Thank you for your letter dated 25th June 1970. I am glad to hear that you have been able to get a job.

The night I had left you at the hotel, late at night the telephone rang. It was your Turtle. Honestly, I got angry and did not tell him in which Hotel you were staying. But, the next morning the hotel keeper told me that Turtle had come in the middle of the night and picked you up and moved you into another hotel. I said to myself, I could not care less. Well I am now glad to see that you are out of Turkey and out of this trouble.

I went to Manavgat yesterday for your hearing. I drove with my car. The hearing was postponed to 20th November 1970 as the court would wait for your birth registration and criminal file or record to be brought from the States. Harika, the wife said that she has gotten 3 more witnesses who knew that you and Süleyman had committed the crime of adultery. The public prosecutor and the judge then decided to call them and get their statements. Süleyman's father told me that he too has hired a lawyer for his son from Manavgat. But, since he had another important case in Alanya, he had today gone to Alanya and would attend the next hearings. I told him that it was not necessary but he did not listen, which means that he has got too much money to spend.

After your papers will be sent from the States, and the three witnesses listened, I think the judge will find out both not guilty. Due to the fact that there is no evidence against you. But, if these new three witnesses say something bad and serious about you, it may change the whole result.

But, even if so there is nothing for you to be afraid of. The decision will not be put to force against you since you are out of Turkey. But the 2,500 liras of bail, may not then be gotten back. But, in any case that money cannot be taken back until the end of the trial. So, you shall have to wait for it patiently. I am afraid the 200 liras I got from you to cover the expenses to come, will exceed and cause us some more expenses. If I succeed to get a decision on your favor then, I shall get these expenses out of this bail and send you the rest only secretly in letters or magazines, since I am not legally allowed to send money out of Turkey by means of official channels. If not you will show me somebody in Turkey to whom I shall pay it. Then that person can pay you back in different currencies.

I helped "Turtle" out with his passport formalities. He is about to get it. But, I am afraid he will have go to Ankara for the necessary Visa. But, that is also very hard to be granted by the Makarios Embassy, as he does not like the Turks. I am sure he will write to you and keep you well informed. He showed me your letters, which proves that you are badly in love with him. All I can say and do is to wish you best of luck and happiness.

The American Consulate did not pay a damn attention to my letter neither to our telephone call. Although he had promised to pay me back the expense of my urgent call, which I later on learned that was 85 liras, they didn't send me a penny. But, I wrote them another, but this time a touching and also a seriously hard letter. Now I am waiting for their response. I hope it will be positive. If not, I shall have to let the other Americans who will have trouble in Turkey, face-to-face with their destiny or bad luck or bad faith.

This is all now, as you know I am busy with my preparations of a journey which I shall leave for, on 28th July to Izmir and from there on by Ferry Boat to Italy and onwards to Austria, Germany, and etc. I shall return in September. So if you want to write me do not write until then.

I know that you could not come to say goodbye to me, because you were ashamed of meeting the Turtle, when you had promised me that you would not. Well this is something you had promised me that you should know and decide. But, I hope you are not making the same mistake *twice. The Turtle is letting his hair grow now. And it has really grown a bit. He says that he shall not return to Turkey, that his father also knows and says "Could not care less." Well, I hope good luck goes with him too.*

Yours sincerely,
Ethan Soykam
Lawyer

***

The following letter was dictated by Süleyman to an unknown tourist who changed the wording (obviously).

Side
August 3, 1970

Dear Karen,

The letters that I have received from you made me very happy—but also sad—for they make the fact that we are now separated (a fact that I can hardly understand) terribly clear to me.

I know of course that I need a visa to go to Cyprus, and as a matter of fact I have already sent my passport to the US Embassy, and according to the man who has helped me there (an American from the embassy, who stayed in my pension), there should be no problems getting the visa. It may arrive any day.

If it were not for these bloody money, I should leave the very day I got the visa, but as I don't know from where I can get those money, I can't tell you when I will be able to come. But one thing is sure. I will come, for I can't live without you.

To live here in Side without you is like Hell. Everything reminds me of you—Side is for me now a town of the dead. Wherever I look I see things that we used to see, when we were together—but your absence has turned these things into razor blades. Side has become a torture chamber.

Separation is a terrible thing, but I feel that our love is so strong that it cannot be destroyed. I love you and I must be with you again. I am going crazy without you. I must see you, I must stay with you. I too want to send you a million of kisses, but what does it help, when I am not there to give them to you.

Write to me, and remember that I love you, and that our bodies and souls, although separated, for me always will be together.

Love,
Süleyman

CHAPTER 19

$\mathcal{H}$elene and I often met to spend our afternoons at the beach in Kyrenia. Our lives were becoming much different. She spent all her time thinking about Muharrem, and never dated anyone. And I was going out with good friends and also on dates, and was slowly and steadily losing my emotions for Süleyman.

Finally at the end of July, Helene, unable to bear being away from Muharrem any longer, returned to Turkey. She and Muharrem stayed together in the little house for a few months. They began saving money for their eventual move to Canada.

I missed Helene, but I found that I was satisfied with my new life in Cyprus. I had no idea how long I'd stay there, but I'd decided just to see what happened and enjoy myself. When I did receive letters from Turkey, though, I would go through a period of sadness and longing for the man I'd loved in that special village, Side, and regret how things had turned out there. I knew I could not return there, ever.

The next letter I received had been dictated to Andrea by Süleyman.

Side
August 8, 1970
Monday

Dear Karen,

My sweet baby, I take your letter few days ago. Now Helene write for me. I don't know you have birthday—sorry. Now Happy Birthday! Helene came to Side but I am too sad because you are not came. I want to see you. I can't stay without you here. I want to come soon to you. But I can't. Because money—money is big problem. You write to me something. You say I don't like you anymore. I am angry because you write like that. Why you write like that? What do you think? I think you said maybe I change but I can't. Because I love you very much. You are my everything! You are my sweet *Bebek [baby]. You know I don't write many letter because I can't write English. But I want you to write every day. If you don't write to me I'm going die. Letter is not enough—I have to see you. Now! But I can't. What I do? I'm goin' crazy here. Help! Bebek! I want to come your little room. I know it very well now. I have a lawyer. I give him 2,000 lira—he do everything about divorce and jail. I don't know how long it will take or what is happening. It doesn't matter if divorce take long time or no. I have just you. You are my everything. I stay in Side but I think every time every minute you. I working hard at Afrodite now—maybe 450 lira. Not much. The radio said the American dollar is worth 15 lira now. Good news. If you think about Side, Side is really change to me. Side is like dead without you. Side is terrible for me. I can't stay more. In Side many girls now, but I can't make something with another girl because you! If it came 1,000, 1,000,000 girl to me, I say no! Because I have a sweet baby.*

I love you.
A thousand million kisses to you from me.
Süleyman XXXXXXXXXXXX

Andrea and Tarik send you their love. They are living in a small house near the beach and are really happy.

Please hurry and write.

Send me a picture please. Soon. XXXXXXXXXXXX

While reading Süleyman's letters, I would feel emotion-sadness, loss. At the same time, I wished he'd find someone else and forget about me. I would sit quietly for awhile, thinking about him and then put the letter down and go on with my life.

***

180

In September, I traveled to Lebanon and Syria with a couple of friends from the UN Peacekeeping Forces. It was an exciting trip for me; I was on the move again, exploring.

Probably my favorite part of that trip was seeing a long camel caravan in the Syrian desert. My friends preferred staying in the Roman ruins in that area, but I took off after the caravan, feeling I'd entered yet another world, a world of centuries past.

CHAPTER 20

O ne September evening, I was entering the discotheque and saw a very handsome man leaning against the entryway pillar. He was tall, dark, and handsome, quite literally. He had an air about him, self-confidence and friendliness. He smiled at me, and I returned the smile.

His name was David, an American who was stationed in Cyprus for three years. The attraction between us was immediate; that night was the beginning of a very serious relationship for us. It also marked the definitive end of my romantic feelings for Süleyman.

I had been keeping my Turkish story from everyone I'd met since I'd arrived in Cyprus. Was I embarrassed and ashamed? Yes. Did I think people would look down on me? Yes.

But David was different. I had a feeling he would understand what happened and still respect me. I wanted him to know everything about me.

So I told him about what happened to me in Turkey. I wasn't surprised when he found the story fascinating and intriguing. And this understanding brought us even closer.

Soon, we rented an apartment and moved in together. We adopted a grey and white kitten. All was going well

And then, in October, my attorney, Mr. Soykam, wrote another letter. I was very impressed by how much Mr. Soykam had done for me.

Ethem Soykam
Avukat
Antalya, Turkey
19/10/1970

Dear Karen,

Thank you for both of your letters. I was indeed glad to hear your good news and the nice progressive feelings and ideas.

I am sorry I could not reply sooner, and I must point out right now here, I shan't be able to write sooner too in the future, apart from the final good news notification. This means that I am much too busy and tired. You know I do not have a secretary also. I thought I had told and informed you of the next trial (hearing) which is due on 20th November 1970. The last time I had gone to the hearing I turned in your application and mine both to the Judge and made him accept that you were discharged from being present at the hearing. Otherwise the judge would have the right of confiscating the 2,000 Turkish Lira bail. But, this money as I have already told you before will not be given back to us until the decision which must be in our favor is finalized. I quite am sure that the wife of Süleyman will appeal to the Supreme Court against the decree of this court, which no doubt will be in our favor. Then this will make us wait for at least another 5–6 months. So, you have to be patient and for the time being forget about this money.

I also remember telling you that the father of Süleyman has hired a lawyer for his son from Manavgat. This is certainly good for us, as he too will defend you and him both and if one is found "Not guilty" the other will be found not guilty too automatically.

I will go to the next hearing (if God is willing). But as you will easily remember my fund for the traveling expenses has ran out. The American consulate replied to me and said that they do not have a special fund for such things. But they were kind enough to send my telephone conversation's bill.

All for now. I hope you do understand that I am very busy. I had a long and very nice journey and vacation in Europe. I took my wife and the two kids and the Ferry-Boat Truva to Brindisi and back. Then I drove to Austria, Germany, Belgium, Holland, France, Switzerland and back to Italy. It lasted 37 days altogether. But, I was terribly tired.

Never mind my silence, you may keep writing and in the meantime you must be reassured that I shall do my best (as I have already done so far) to protect your rights.

Until then, I send you my best wishes and I am yours,

Sincerely,
Ethem Soykam
Your Attorney

***

The next letter was dictated to Ian and reworded by him. I had written to Süleyman, trying to explain to him that I'd fallen in love with an American man. This was Süleyman's final letter to me.

October 21, 1970

Dear Karen,

I think you should remember me—Ian—we came from Nicosia to Adana and Adana to Side together in June—OK.

Süleyman: I'm sorry I've not written for so long a time—I've had nobody to write a letter for me. I'm very unhappy because I didn't understand your last letter properly, but I think I understand now and you want to finish with me. Please come and see me again after the trial (in a month's time). Then we can talk together and understand each other. I still love you very much and think of you all the time.

The American boy you write about—are you sleeping with him or is he only a friend? Do you want to finish with me because of this boy or is it because you don't love me anymore?

If you are coming to Turkey, write to me first so that I will be expecting you. I don't have a girlfriend at all except you and it's only you that I love. Here in Side, we have a good life. You must come back and share it with me. Soon all the trouble will be finished—I've stayed a long time now for four months waiting for you. I like you very much but if you say you want to finish I don't say anything just "Fuck you bastard!" Why do I say this to you—because we have big problems—we are much stronger than these problems—the problems finish now and you say you want to finish. But I can say this to you because I love you and if you love me you write a letter to me and tell me everything.

I'm really angry with you because you write like that—but why—I don't understand. But I think you find this American son-of-a-bitch boy—because of him you say it doesn't matter anymore about me. I want you to remember all the time that I love you

184

Süleyman

Ian: I'm here for a few weeks so I'll read any letters you send to Süleyman and make sure he understands.

After reading the above letter, I then wrote to Süleyman, doing my best to explain my feelings for David. I told Süleyman I would always cherish the time I'd spent with him. I thanked Ian for being there to explain all this to him.

Anyone who reads my story would probably wonder why I didn't just break up with Süleyman when I left Turkey. Or better yet, why did I continue with Süleyman in Turkey when I realized I didn't really want to have a future with him.

The truth is – I don't know the answer for sure. However, the more I've continued to learn about myself, the more I realize I hold on to the one I have until I have another.

This is ugly. And immature, but it's clear to me now that I've done this again and again.

***

By April 1971, both David and I knew we had a great relationship. We understood each other very well and enjoyed our life together. We got married in Nicosia, a very casual wedding at the office of the justice of the peace with two of our friends as witnesses. I left my discotheque job and became a stay-at-home wife. I learned to cook fantastic Middle Eastern food and sewed most of my clothes. We adopted a gray-and-white kitten. Our free time was spent exploring the island, the mountains, the coast, and the villages. Cyprus is a gorgeous island; we enjoyed every minute we spent there.

I kept thinking about what had happened in Turkey, though. Not wanting to forget anything, I rented a manual typewriter and spent hours at our kitchen table writing what you're reading now. My intention was to keep this as a diary for myself and then give it to my family as a gift.

My mother had sent me all the letters I'd written to the family, which I added to the story. Then what I wrote traveled with me for decades and sat on my bookshelves wherever I lived. It's only now, years later, that I've decided to share this story with others.

The trial in Turkey continued for over a year and at long last Süleyman and I were found "not guilty". The following are Mr. Soykam's final letters to me.

***

The following are all letters from Mr. Soykam.

Ethem Soykam
Avukat
Antalya, Turkey
26 June 1971

Dear Karen,

Here I am at long last on the spotlight for the final good news. Yes, the trial has come to an end and you were both found not guilty. Because of the mistakes you two have had done during the early stages of the inquisitions, I had to provide some more and new witnesses and make it really clear that you had not gotten beyond the friendly relations which is normally seen and found in a place which is the center of tourism; in other words, a summer resort like Side. To achieve this happy end, I went to the court (for the hearings) 6 more times. Chronologically the dates were as follows:

19th/6/1970
17th/7/1970
20th/11/1970
12th/3/1971
16th/6/1971

But, after the last hearing I did not yet go to Manavgat. I will have to go during the coming week again and find out whether she has appealed to the Supreme Court within 7 days after the verdict (decision) was announced. If she does, then the decision will not be finalized and we will have to wait until it is approved and certified. Then we will be able to get the bail back. In my former letter, I later on saw that I have written it 2,000 liras, by mistake.

Now, you must be happy to hear this good news of mine, and rest relieved as I had told you from the very beginning and send by inform me about how to send the rest of the 2,500 liras for you after deducting my expenses, costs, etc.

You have seen it with your own eyes that a hearing takes a whole day of mine. I did not book a taxi, as I had my car and since there was no more funds left to cover my necessary expenses after the hearing I would either go to Side to have a fish or dine in Manavgat. For a total amount of 6 times going and coming to Manavgat and including two more times to go in the car and funds for gasoline etc. I should say that I will charge you altogether one and a half thousand liras. The remaining amount of 1,000 liras (if you are not willing to give me a little more tip) I will send or give as you say and desire. In my file, I have an amount of 343 lira debit on your account too, after the American General Consul's refusal of paying the pertaining expenses. If you like in two separate letters I will airmail you 1,000 Turkish liras in two [five-hundred-dollar] banknotes. But, I am afraid the Greeks may search our letters sent from Turkey. If you have a friend in England, Germany or elsewhere I can send the letters to that address and from there, they will be forwarded to your address. This time I will do a favor for you and send this 1,010 Turkish liras without the decision's getting finalized.

PS: Süleyman's wife was very upset and angry with me to hear the decision. She called all of us bad names and cursed us. Süleyman is as you left him. Doing nothing and sometimes fighting with Ali for women and girls. I shall go away in August for vacation.

***

Athene Motel
Side, telefon; 17—Antalya

10th July 1971

Dear Karen,

Firstly, I heartily congratulate you for your "approved" marriage and wish you long-life happiness.

Secondly I congratulate both of us and inform you of the unexpected reaction of Harika appealing to the Supreme Court against the decree. Thus, the decree is now finalized.

To-day taking advantage of being Saturday, and having no hearing I drove to Manavgat, went to the court, found out all these and after a lot of waiting and overcoming the difficult formalities, I was able to draw the money, just before the bank was closed at 13.30.

I am (before leaving for my vacation) going to send your promised money to your husband's address. But, I wondered if you are planning to come to Antalya will you not be needing that money anyway and anyhow? Therefore if you say that I should keep it until you come, I shall do so, if you say that I should mail them to two separate envelopes, I will do as you say.

I am writing this letter, after I had my lunch in this new Motel of Side (very near Turtel). This is rather far and out from Side and should you decide to spend a few days at a quiet sea-side, it is most suitable. Life is still the same in Side, the same kind of life for those people too. Unless the village is not moved out of its old place or foreigners come, settle and change their rather primitive and superstitious life and beliefs, they will no doubt remain the same. So, do not feel sorry or pity for any one. Especially Süleyman as he has turned out to be a woman-chaser. But something rather strange about him, he seems to have something "secret maybe" to offer or give to the female sex. But that only is of course not enough.

We will be very happy to see you in Antalya and to meet your husband. Tell him that he can easily take me as his best man in his (past) wedding. Well, all for now please acknowledge receipt of my letter and its first enclosure, by return of mail. Then I will mail the other piece. Until then, take care, God bless you both and give you good, healthy children.

With my sincere and warm regards,

I am yours,
Very sincerely.

***

E. Soykam
2nd September 1971

Dear Karen,

I got your letter when I returned from my vacation and I was glad to hear that you received my earlier letter safely. I hope you will receive this one safely too.

I am enclosing the last obligation of mine. I wish to rest assured that I have done an excellent job for you and consequently rendered a most satisfying service. Please write and inform your arrival in Antalya beforehand so that I can be in Antalya. Maybe there might be a few items I might ask you to kindly bring for me. Also do not forget to inform me of your receipt of this letter of mine, so that I shall not be kept worried.

We are all well. The journey was O.K. despite a traffic accident in which I participated. My car was damaged and caused and costed me about 200 dollars repair. Thank God nothing happened to us.

Best of luck to you and your husband, and best wishes, with sincerest warm regards.

Yours very sincerely,

EK

As Mr. Soykam wrote, the decree had been finalized. I was very happy and relieved.

But was it really "finished"? Not yet.

Slowly, a desire built up in my mind. I realized there was one thing left for me to do before I'd be satisfied.

EPILOGUE

Yes, I needed to return to Turkey. And it was David who realized this need of mine and suggested it first.

`When we were preparing to leave Cyprus in 1973, he suggested going to Turkey, and certainly Side, so he could see where I'd had my adventures and so I could see once again the place where I'd lived through such a drama.

"It can be the first stop on our trip to North Africa," he suggested.

I hesitated. And I continued to hesitate for a while. Did I dare to return to Turkey? Hadn't I sworn I'd never, ever go back there?

Yes, I had promised myself to stay away from that country forever.

However, I started reconsidering. First, I have to admit I was curious to return, to see how I felt about the place now. I also really wanted David to see all the places I'd described to him. *Would it really be dangerous?* I wondered. After all, Süleyman and I had been acquitted. The facts of the case had been sealed. I had no more romantic feelings for Süleyman, and I was sure our feelings were mutual. And I'd be with David.

So David and I decided to go. We were prepared to leave Side immediately if there were any bad feelings at all.

But we needn't have worried for even a minute.

We arrived in Side and found a room in Dogan's pension. The first morning we were there, Süleyman walked up to us while we were having coffee in one of the restaurants. He was quite friendly. During the week, we spent quite a bit of time together, along with a bunch of other tourists and Turks. We also spent an afternoon at Süleyman's brother's house. Süleyman's father treated us to çay at the coffeehouse.

During the time I had been away from Turkey, Side had changed a lot. The village had become more commercialized and a little Westernized. Some Turkish women were even going around in knee-length dresses without pajamas, and many of the men were wearing more modern dress. A couple of small advertising signs were hanging in the square. Work was being done on some more motels to line the beaches. Süleyman's brother had converted his tiny house into a pension, and his family was living in one room in the basement. The money fever had hit, which made me very sad. Side was still nothing like a typical tourist town, though. It was still a small village with its traditional ways, but I wondered how long it would remain that way.

The day my husband and I left Side, we headed for Antalya to wait for our flight to Istanbul. And there was Süleyman on the main street—whether accidentally or purposefully, I'll never know. We all went to a movie that evening, and he treated us to pastries and *salep* (a hot drink made from dried tubers of orchids). After that visit, my husband I felt ashamed that we'd doubted Süleyman for a minute or worried at all about our visit to Side. Both of us felt quite fond of him and his family, and both of us were genuinely sad to tell him goodbye. He told us that day that he wanted to work in Austria and that he was working on papers to allow him to go there. Who knows if he did? I question it, knowing his feeling about work. But maybe he's changed.

At the Antalya airport, David grabbed my hand. "Are you satisfied now, Karen? Do you feel everything worked out well?" he asked me.

"Yes," I replied, smiling at him. "It couldn't have been better. We, together, were welcomed to my favorite Turkish village by people I really care about. There was no anger, no jealousy—just friendliness and *smiles*. It was wonderful!"

After our stay in Cyprus and visit to Turkey, my husband was posted to other countries And our foreign adventures continued.

CPSIA information can be obtained
at www.ICGtesting.com
Printed in the USA
BVHW080936170323
660662BV00002B/333